Past Life Regression

How to Guide Yourself Back to the Past

(A Complete Self Help Workbook on Past Life Healing Dowsing Technique)

Zachary Minton

Published By **John Kembrey**

Zachary Minton

All Rights Reserved

Past Life Regression: How to Guide Yourself Back to the Past (A Complete Self Help Workbook on Past Life Healing Dowsing Technique)

ISBN 978-1-7779561-3-4

No part of this guidebook shall be reproduced in any form without permission in writing from the publisher except in the case of brief quotations embodied in critical articles or reviews.

Legal & Disclaimer

The information contained in this book is not designed to replace or take the place of any form of medicine or professional medical advice. The information in this book has been provided for educational & entertainment purposes only.

The information contained in this book has been compiled from sources deemed reliable, and it is accurate to the best of the Author's knowledge; however, the Author cannot guarantee its accuracy and validity and cannot be held liable for any errors or omissions. Changes are periodically made to this book. You must consult your doctor or get professional medical advice before using any of the suggested remedies, techniques, or information in this book.

Upon using the information contained in this book, you agree to hold harmless the Author from and against any damages, costs, and expenses, including any legal fees potentially resulting from the application of any of the information provided by this guide. This disclaimer applies to any damages or injury caused by the use and application, whether directly or indirectly, of any advice or information presented, whether for breach of contract, tort, negligence, personal injury, criminal intent, or under any other cause of action.

You agree to accept all risks of using the information presented inside this book. You need to consult a professional medical practitioner in order to ensure you are both able and healthy enough to participate in this program.

Table Of Contents

Chapter 1: Fascination 1

Chapter 2: A Calling To Remember 4

Chapter 3: How Does Religion Work Into This? 8

Chapter 4: Is It Wrong To Recall Your Past Lives? 14

Chapter 5: How To Recall Your Own Past Lives Without Seeking 18

Chapter 6: How To Trust Your Memories When 33

Chapter 7: How To Tell If Your Memory Is Real 40

Chapter 8: Reasons You Can't Remember 44

Chapter 9: How Does All This Help You With Your Awakening? 57

Chapter 10: Prompts To Help Jog Your Memory 60

Chapter 11: How To Know You Experiencing A Spiritual Awakening 70

Chapter 12: The Intriguing Concept Of Past Lives 74

Chapter 13: The Soul Clocks 87

Chapter 14: Echo Encounters 98

Chapter 15: The Evidence For Regression 111

Chapter 16: The Enigma Of Reincarnation 123

Chapter 17: Scientific Revelations 136

Chapter 18: Psychology And Regression 149

Chapter 19: Regression Therapy 162

Chapter 20: Emerging Memories 175

Chapter 1: Fascination

It's outstanding to have even one memory! To have a memory is not just a reminiscence which include you recalling your teenagers; it is an active recording of your past. It surfaces with a powerful feeling of recollection and familiarity. And if you gain this without a doubt, then that is a part of you from the better geographical areas! You'll never have the ability to remember a past existence in case you're no longer intended to Or now not supposed to don't forget that existence in question.

You can revel in the reminiscence floor as it raises up from in which it is stored to your soul. And this is furthermore similarly affirmation to you that your soul exists! Also that is an example of techniques our souls, minds, hearts, chakras and bodily our our bodies all artwork collectively to get us through bodily life on Earth.

It's furthermore charming because we're capable of see how we did NOT go to hell for religious crimes we did not realise we had been committing and we were given some exceptional danger to hook up with the souls of that life and ensure we understood our commands and completed any karmic problems which have been keeping us again.

Lastly, our souls are actual, living, respiratory beings other than our bodily bodies. Our souls are strength and at the same time as strength does now not "breathe" it does take information and emotional experience from each breath your bodily frame takes. While in lifestyles, we have an internal map that leads us thru our lives. And the reality that we want to take into account a past lifestyles in any respect, says lots about what our souls are honestly asking us.

When you have got an urge to keep in mind a past life, that is your soul seeking to get your interest to put together to research, develop or transition into a lesson or karmic state of affairs to paintings via. Because of this, I urge you to no longer be in a rush to "awaken." Sometimes, that allows you to wake up, we ought to clean out vintage energies that allows you to increase our vibration.

The deeper reason people are searching out the capacity to preserve in mind them is due to the reality you've got got the capability to peer which you are in reality an eternal being that has lengthy long gone into the mild and been reborn more than one times. In this awakening, you've got got get right of entry to to the most profound lesson you can ever observe! And that is at the equal time as you begin to recognize what real countless slight, intelligence, and what infinite love in reality is.

The deliver of our souls is that this infinite love and facts. This is wherein we came from, and wherein we constantly return to.

Chapter 2: A Calling To Remember

If you're asking approximately recalling your past lives and to procure this e-book, and in social media groups in search of solutions, probabilities are you are trying to answer an internal calling to remember. But, you are no longer definitely asking to don't forget, you are asking to get assist to discover your root of being. Your soul. Your better self is directing you to discover the difference among your soul and your physical body! And at the same time as we try this, we're entering into the number one tiers of a new soul growth. And so, the following lesson is what to look for on your soul growth. Why are we searching for this?

LOVE

This phrase is tough. For the record, I'm regarding love the strength in region of affection the emotion. But this doesn't imply that every don't move into this communicate. Many humans begin their spiritual trips with a immoderate approach and don't comprehend that they're missing the opportunity to truely recognize what supply is prepared to tell them. In order to certainly increase spiritually, you continue to want to recognize love for what it's miles! Love is likewise an historical word for energy and it's furthermore every other way to provide an explanation for the power of fact. And not simply truth, but countless popularity that we are following through our instinct. Following your coronary coronary heart is a actual coaching that during reality does mean to concentrate for your inner voice and internal know-how. Seeking your past existence memories is in a way, attempting to connect with this inner information. So, you really need to take a look at your heart with the intention to experience the reminiscences you have got stored inside you.

How did you get "Love" out of Past existence recollection? How did this get weird?

It's no longer simply. When you first ground yourself, and 2d, apprehend in reality the infinity that is our higher selves, you begin to start to apprehend how restricted our human minds clearly are and the manner massive our souls truely are that the bare eye can't see before everything.

The reality approximately compassion is that it's far OK to are trying to find it, feel it and explicit it. And it's far OK to give it to others that do not align together with your beliefs. The truth is, the area your higher self comes from does no longer realise anger, judgment, hate or violence. It ought to not recognize guilt, or complaint or correction other than at the same time as you need to understand your feature in abuse brought about in the direction of others. All the horrible you deliver others, is not out of your god self, or your coronary heart. It's from your ego. Source, or God, does NOT have an ego.

So, recalling your past lives is lots more than just what it looks like. It's a glimpse into the lively global this is our higher life. It's wherein we began, and in which we're going. And at the same time as we "wake up" and realize we've got come over again, we see that that is proper.

Love is the sum of all things. While we are alive inside the world, we're reduce off from the alternative detail it really is our particular source. This source is in a experience hidden from us whilst we paintings our way thru existence in darkness. We can pick out out to get right of entry to it via prayer, meditation, desires, or possibly contemplation.

Chapter 3: How Does Religion Work Into This?

This is one of the maximum hard factors of teaching this difficulty! Everyone has a extremely good factor of view, follows a high-quality church with taken into consideration one in every of a kind guidelines, or over assumes that the priority of reincarnation can not be blended with faith, or there can be an excessive amount of religion concerned inside the trouble. They thru a few method must separate beyond life recollection proper right into a unique container than the simplest that they have got been raised with. This isn't always genuine.

One of the advantages of recalling your beyond lives is seeing the reality for what it's miles and mastering in which religion and spirituality certainly healthy into the large image. In lots of my memories I can hold in thoughts the slight organising for me and me going into it with out loads as a request for repentance or a want to save you and pray to ensure I get access. The slight in reality opens and I move in.

This doesn't suggest that religion is related to the white mild, or that it isn't always. And I can also keep in mind the angels that got here to me to help me in crossing over. Again, they did no longer request repentance or prayer and I simply went in. Sometimes the angels got here and assisted me without saying one word to me! So, this can pleasant propose that they are for absolutely everyone and constantly proper here to assist! And it's that clean. Because I ought to undergo in mind seeing them, I understood this early in my life. This opened any other "forbidden field" that I changed into taught should anger God if I seemed in it. And that is that if the angels are continuously there for us, then so is God, supply, the writer and also you get the concept. But is that this due to the reality I usual the perception that God exists? Was I forced to peer this and take shipping of it?

No! It technique that we choose out lives with the information we want to revel in. We pick out out out our religion, or to be atheist. Our souls are not non secular the least bit! We are essentially spirit in bodily bodies until we select out to practice a faith at the same time as in our lives. We are electricity returning to power. The divine mind and coronary coronary coronary heart is our parent power. It's our preference to make it non secular. Do you word what I'm seeking to provide an reason behind? You can actually see God as actually strength and mild and nothing else.

The truth is, when you have skilled a beyond lifestyles reminiscence earlier than, you have got already seen this. Our souls continuously re-align with the moderate each time we move over and it is natural and pure. It's our maximum fact.

The only manner to check this for your self, is to sense it inner your being. Sit in a quiet place and ask yourself this query and notice what the response is.

Religion is amazing defined as a set of hints created thru a spiritual agency. If your intestine is to comply with the ones guidelines, then that is a preference you made on your lifestyles plan. The divine thoughts and coronary heart works every strategies.

SO, DOES THIS MEAN THAT YOU DON'T NEED TO BE RELIGIOUS TO EXPERIENCE YOUR SPIRITUAL AWAKENING?

No! Not the least bit! Though many humans start off as devout church goers, once you begin to delve into recalling your past lives and also you start to get the finer facts of among lives, you notice how massive and endless deliver in reality is. The number one motive we are taught to choose religion is to hold our souls from judgment. But as soon as we examine that divine love doesn't determine, this modifications the script and lets in us see the bigger photo and that our souls are limitless as properly. This is the start of our awakening.

This maintains as we learn how to experience the vibration of truth. A beyond life reminiscence may be felt and on occasion, it could be felt in advance than you can take into account it. When you can endure in thoughts a beyond life, you could moreover experience a "waking up" feeling. This will vibrate and FEEL proper.

It will revel in which encompass you fell asleep even as your final life ended and you wakened on this lifestyles as although it's a brand new day. You FEEL this. It's now not certainly a reminiscence or a hallucination. It's an inner expertise. And the primary a part of a fact approximately you that you could locate that resonates so strongly which you can't bypass over it.

Chapter 4: Is It Wrong To Recall Your Past Lives?

Hopefully, you don't assume so after the ultimate paragraph, however we had been conditioned to ignore our inner selves all through our lives. So we'll communicate this.

First, it is herbal and masses of can try this without any try. If it turn out to be unnatural, we wouldn't be capable of in any respect. And therefore, this statistics might not be to be had. The higher thoughts, or the God mind, or infinite mind, gave us all the gadget to apprehend and get via existence which includes the existing of spirituality and the capability to "wake ourselves" up. Why could a author forbid it but provide us the ability to do it? To mess with us? To restrict us? No. Our god/creator can't be greater restrained than we are. This is likewise your evidence that there may be an smart being at the foundation of our universe.

There is NO RULE at the manner to place you in any form of "religious jeopardy" so as to harm your soul if we're to head on the phrase of keyboard "religious" warriors or the ones properly which means friends that seem practical to us. The rule of endless knowledge and love quality courses us to our extremely good pastimes continually.

But, there's a problem about residing vs recalling to have a look at. Let's define this.

Dwelling: Means to live in a notion manner or on an idea for a completely excessively long time.

To day dream.

Recalling to have a look at:

To take active steps to understand an energetic issue, karmic state of affairs, or experience an awakening.

This is what I am teaching you to apprehend nowadays.

If you awaken and you may endure in mind a beyond existence memory, you're now not living on it. Don't panic, and do now not try and stifle it. Write it down. This isn't the same factor as living! You have been supposed to recollect this memory inside the suggest time. It has a vibration of truth to it. A beyond life reminiscence is unmistakable! It's now not like recalling wherein you left some element out of a recipe.

There must be a stability of time used to try this. You ought to now not spend all day in this in case you start to write down your reminiscences as they floor. But, this is going with the whole thing you are taking on. You ought to no longer spend all day cooking, or all day on the seashore, or all day gaming, or all day in your garden. That's simply not unusual revel in. There isn't any harm in looking for a beyond existence memory but, a few information aren't as vital as others.

Some lives we recall sincerely to expose us that we have "woken up" in a new existence and survived the lack of life we also can were fearful of in our past existence and not whatever extra.

Some lives we recall right inside the mean time the lesson started so we can try to apprehend it another time. Fact, the word "sin" technique to miss your mark. So sinning is missing the opportunity to study a lesson this is in the front folks, not pleasant a horrible mistake that we were taught to worry.

Chapter 5: How To Recall Your Own Past Lives Without Seeking

A SPIRITUALIST OR HYPNOTIST

This can take a few attempt for a few humans. I had been able to use those techniques thinking about my children and I definitely have identified this with others and attempted to provide an explanation for what they had been experiencing.

Journaling approximately a specific element you're inquisitive about. Ex. Greek meals, Irish step dancing. You need to first experience the attraction to this object. Roman columns, the sea, ect. It can be tedious and time eating. The trick is to attend till you experience a second of know-how toward a person or a detail.

Ex. You're at art work and you're speakme to the state-of-the-art worker and also you get alongside right now. You experience drawn to them almost like a sibling or great friend. This is in which you will write down your emotions and what includes thoughts. Journaling can assist the power go together with the go with the flow.

A phrase of caution:

Because plenty folks typically have a tendency to enjoy feelings toward a person that may be overwhelming or which consist of you're assembly your best pal all all over again, I will provide this word of caution. If you're reading this, you're already properly on your way on your religious awakening in any other case you experience that deep reference to some different soul. You're in all likelihood beforehand of the game and they may enjoy their kinship in the direction of you however might not apprehend it but. I implore you to be diffused approximately the problem and keep soul searching out your element of the relationship. For some purpose many humans misunderstand the message from the universe being introduced through distinct awakening souls and in area of preventing to experience it out, they near their minds. It looks like commonplace experience to some of us, however the ego is a difficult block to art work with. Simply take it one step at a time and follow your instinct to be as genuine a chum as you could for that 2nd and each second you're given. Be thankful and they'll take a look at their very very own inner voice with what's written for your divine plan with them. This is the maximum crucial issue in any karmic bond. Don't push them to undergo in mind in the event that they're now not showing an openness to apprehend if you've given hints. You want to understand that in case you are destined to be more than buddies, you may be!

Also, in instances like these, do not ask approximately if they may be capable of bear in mind you in case you do bear in mind a reminiscence. Simply be there and gift, excellent, sympathetic and peaceful. Foster a modern-day friendship first. There's an unusual stigma associated with talking approximately beyond lives that has a tendency to push over thinkers into the opportunity mind-set and plenty of humans may not but be able to see the larger photograph like you could. If they ask you first, then preserve with the conversation however however take it lightly.

1. As stated, the biggest indicator is the manner you experience about a situation. This isn't always coming out of your mind, but your soul. Feel this out. Your instinct will guide you however take it slow. You can feel the information of a situation. Also, pay attention to yourself and your internal voice. Sometimes terms like "brother", "father", "aunt", or perhaps "sister" will ground in regard to the character. Sometimes you may pay attention your self remember unique phrases which incorporates "This I won't fall for..." or "This time I'll inform them I love them..." Many instances your memory will communicate to you. You will listen your internal self telling

you what you don't forget from the closing lifestyles if you are listening.

2. Pay attention to your goals. Past lives will floor via your desires. And they will be hard to use a dream dictionary on. Follow your instincts and write those down and maintain them in a magazine. This will take area even as you are in an possibility to healing the lesson you not noted formerly or if you have a brand new soul connection coming in.

3. In addition to people that you straight away sense associated with, humans that you routinely do not like for no motive are a signal that you lived a beyond existence with them. This is a strong indicator of karma that you are approximately to approach. This is in which you ask, "Was I bullied? Was I the trouble? Do I owe this man or woman an apology? Do they owe me an apology?" Spend a while in your mind with this man or woman and supply it some concept. What does your

coronary coronary heart inform you to restore? Try to keep a peaceful mind-set as you continue. You do now not need a lousy relationship to dominate your existence. Take it slow and give gratitude for the lesson and do your excellent to remedy it as definitely as possible. Or steer easy in case your gut tells you to perform that.

four. Pay interest to the manner your head buzzes or the woosh or woozy emotions you will possibly get on the equal time as you're round someone you sense acquainted with. Our souls launch antique electricity this way.

I commenced experiencing the use of tension a few years inside the beyond once I were travelling effortlessly for years! And at extremely good points, I'd flat out just begin spontaneously panicking whilst the usage of! This modified into not like me! It took some GENTLE tries however I in the end had been given the memory of looking for to interrupt out a poisonous relationship and ultimately loss of life because of it, to floor in whole coloration! And I observed heaps more approximately my existence lesson and a centuries vintage emotional connection that I have become caught in! I'm proud to say that my anxiety has began out to vanish and I'm nearly able to adventure peacefully another time.

Step thru way of step:

1. When you start to enjoy an emotion which include fear, anger, or maybe strong familiarity toward a person or some element definitely take a few deep breaths and mentally count on or say to your self, "I permit this memory to ground." Make extraordinary you ask gently and peacefully and then clearly permit your mind to wander or be curious.

2. Pay attention to any sensations you feel together with surprising anxiety, disappointment or like your hobby is being pulled towards a part of your body. You also

can moreover want to repeat this some times as a few reminiscences are buried or in a manner, caught down deep. You might also furthermore enjoy your head buzzing , or like a strain is trying to release.

three. Take a deep breath and recognition on it and visualize this memory taking walks its way upwards.

If now not a few issue comes up, your emotions could in all likelihood best need to be felt. But lighten up and live affected individual. Allow yourself to sense them and remind yourself of the subsequent:

I'm safe. I'm in a new life now. This situation is over. It is freeing. I'm now permitting it to release.

I allow this to floor and I ask for a moderate launch please. (cognizance cause in your higher self, your publications or angels)

Be grateful.

Again, you can need to repeat this a few instances. Sit quietly and repeat taking deep breaths and set your motive on releasing it.

I actually have had severa buddies talk to me overtly about lives we shared collectively and whole in facts that I in no way had to inform them approximately first. Lives in Ancient Egypt, The Early 13 Colonies, World War II, and Medieval Eurpope to name a few. I as soon as had a co-employee walk as masses as me and begin the conversation as inquire from me first if I remembered her! I did! I grow to be extremely joyful and excited and we talked like we were antique buddies, which we were! This is due to the truth your reminiscences are a fact that you study and experience like a map!

The most recovery lifestyles I can bear in mind, surfaced only some weeks earlier than I commenced this ebook. I had began to enjoy excessive tension at the same time as the usage of just a few years in the past whilst I had a sense it have become probably from past karma, I had started out out to marvel if it turn out to be genetic. I observed all the steps above and I ought to experience it seeking to ground but it wouldn't budge for weeks! And the worst detail became that it grow to be seeking to ground at some point of instances once I emerge as busy.

Finally one night time I changed into relaxed and laying in mattress and on the point of sleep and the memory in query surfaced like I had virtually had a fundamental dream! I can also moreover want to see the economic organization walls, and pay interest my communication with the economic organization personnel and I knew this end up it! I permit it play out like scene in a film (that i had never seen) and i observed the factor in which I knew I needed to release and this was while a member of the family had positioned me down and harm me and stored me from developing up and I wasn't allowed some component more than number one room and board in that existence! It changed into sad and I wasn't even allowed to mourn the lack of my freedom!

The feeling slowly and peacefully came to thoughts and I determined out that I changed into now allowed to permit this cross!

A few weeks in the beyond, I became the usage of domestic and felt a compulsion to take note of an antique tune associated with a memory and while I couldn't don't forget the whole reminiscence I did enjoy the disappointment and allowed myself to release it privately and legitimately cry about it which in no way happens!

Whether you preserve in thoughts the entire memory or experience it, write it down. Don't be too adamant on searching for to keep in mind it if it received't ground however you may enjoy it. Some lives aren't meant to be completely recalled. But this is essentially it. Time, endurance, and allowing your self to endure in mind.

WHEN YOUR MEMORIES FULLY SURFACE

Your reminiscences can floor gently and in entire colour or they're capable of ground short and in a surprising whoosh out of your feet in your head! I've had every take place! You might in all likelihood enjoy a de javu, or an uncertainty. If you lived a exquisite lifestyles with a person you are remembering, you could sense wonder pleasure or an unexplainable happy feeling! Our souls understand earlier than we can consciously understand.

Now that I defined the ones techniques, I want to provide an cause for a way to get your reminiscences in a piece extra element. But I suppose it's far important to discuss the manner to simply accept as genuine with what you're seeing as a reminiscence vs what your mind has the energy to create.

WHAT TO DO WHEN THEY ARE TRAUMATIC MEMORIES

To repeat, ensure you pay attention for your inner voice and your ego. If you experience afraid of this lifestyles in search of to return thru your soul's memory, take a deep breath and repeat what you truly have a look at. Take it gradual with this. Remember that not something can harm you again and that you are safe and in a modern existence. I without a doubt have had dreams approximately the Salemn witch trials which have been demanding on the time, but now they're no longer whatever to consider due to the fact I want to keep in mind why it passed off and who became right and who modified into incorrect. And I had already become assured that I became going to be OK.

Now in very uncommon instances, you may undergo in mind a lifestyles that you haven't sincerely certainly finished but and because of this that you have an attachment from that life. And which means the soul of some other man or woman has been following you from this lifestyles and inflicting contamination or nightmares. I can first-class preference that I end up the ONLY character that expert this, but because of the reality I'm human and I need to recall wondering that I preferred to repair this karma for myself as a little one, I want to expect that others may too. And permit me simply say this, that very vintage souls will constantly act wiser their years and now and again communicate like an adult even as they'll be youngsters. This does NOT recommend they have all the answers but it does suggest they may be really capable of information advanced ideas like what we're discussing right here. Do not panic if your kids speak this manner. It's precise element and it could make your machine as a discern much less complex.

If you keep in thoughts a past existence and discover which you have an attachment, my most powerful concept is to are seeking for Reiki restoration from a practitioner and ask your publications and angels for assist in this. Ask them to every dispose of the energy themselves or to manual to you to a reputable practitioner. Read reviews while looking online. Plus the Reiki practitioner is probably in a function that will help you understand this reminiscence better and release it lots faster. And this could be a motive that a stressful life may not floor in a entire shade like others would probable. To protect you. But another time, this is very unusual and now not a not unusual hassle, but I without a doubt have seen it rise up for the few people that I even have talked to.

Chapter 6: How To Trust Your Memories When

THEY SURFACE

Well, as I've been pronouncing, you can generally sense the reality whilst you permit yourself to perform that. But, for humans who've hassle trusting their intuition or gut feelings, the undertaking of all topics supernatural, angels, reincarnation, ghosts or a few problem else, has a tendency to get pigeonholed into a magical fairytale document of "first rate but now not actual." And after this, the mind will disregard with, "our minds have to make up stuff whilst we need it that badly." This is in thing due to the fact we don't want others to decide us, we don't need to be incorrect, or we don't need to appear ignorant or loopy. This is the ego's voice strolling to protect us from something that it thinks must get us unfairly judged and therefore take away our ability to stay on. Anything regarding a fear is the ego looking for to help us get thru bodily existence. And alas, it could be overzealous and knock us off course from what we want to apprehend.

So, what do you agree with you studied? Is it actual? What do you receive as genuine with you studied will arise if you ask your self this? I say this due to the fact everyone have souls on journeys. And all anyone has to do is achieve into the self and experience for the reality. Our minds are certainly very powerful and high-quality we're able to create some matters out of wishful questioning, however while turn out to be the last time you created a fake memory to assuage your revel in of wonder and hobby?

Typically we create fake memories after best mind injuries or highbrow issues form. If you do not have this, or in no way had this hassle before, it's miles no longer the "trick."

I as soon as had a woman strive to tell me that my psychic capability modified into in truth choosing up on pics from different humans's travels.

And I right away had a memory surface of a existence in which I had this potential and I allowed another who did now not recognize to tell me I imagined it! I vowed in that life prolonged prolonged in the past that I might in no way allow every different soul to try to stifle my potential and my proper self ever once more! I felt that she changed into incorrect and I have emerge as truly doing the right issue with the aid of way of acknowledging my beyond existence memories. Your past existence reminiscences are like a ebook or a historic report deep for your soul. You can FEEL them.

Why is it precious at the way to allow yourself to don't forget your beyond life memories?

For the subsequent, honestly due to the fact I'm speakme approximately "God" does no longer mean I'm talking about church or faith. As I noted previously, the non secular archetype you have were given been raised to fear isn't the not unusual intelligence or coronary heart that I'm referring to for this e-book. All references of God are implying the later.

1. You can see the existence of your soul. By recalling and trusting what your seeing, you can feel your very personal spirit and attention. And consequently, you ultimately see the lifestyles of God.

2. You start to permit drift of the concern of the religious archetypes collectively with displeasing God and being punished with Hell. The constrained thoughts expands to really see truely how endless the universe honestly is.

3. You begin to see which you're strolling thru your errors and that you're allowed to lead them to. And you're lovely and allowed to be cherished. Love is the

power that resonates via out our global and universe. People select and preserve anger.

four. You start your spiritual awakening. And your soul starts offevolved to enlarge in vibration at the same time as you count on this like to fill your life.

five. You see all of your troubles as quick. Nothing is all of the time.

6. You see all of your life route options.

7. You can see in which your relationships may be healed or in which you hold choosing abusive or toxic relationships and you turn out to be more conscious of them and begin make adjustments.

eight. You need to understand what's subsequent, and a way to reach for higher and make your life higher and begin to looking for to accomplish that, or are seeking out greater gratifying possibilities.

9. You emerge as stronger in your self.

10. You start to understand the fact approximately how love surely works. When a trusted authority parent along with a figure or boss offers you ultimatums and tells you life received't enhance, or you are stuck. This is not real! Compassion is in ample supply and all you want to do is search for it and ask for it.

11. In a number of my past lives, I honestly have very clean memories of the angels that helped me pass over. You no longer best get your evidence that god is actual, but that angels exist and are continually with us. They in no way select out, by no means condemn, and I've always been handled the identical on the cease of every life via a massive adorable white light and the angels inclined to help me to move over. This has been the identical fact for all my lives and has in no manner modified! They are constantly with us with love and recognize and without a call for for reward or repentance.

There is a big amount of facts available every immediately and not right now due to recalling our past lives. My maximum preferred lesson about reincarnation is that if my soul comes returned, then I can't be destroyed. This technique my soul is limitless. This method your soul is limitless. This is the likeness we have been created in. God is endless and now not first-rate this, however clever beyond comprehension. Infinite and countless in love and forgiveness. And if you could collect this and you do, then you may deliver it. If you're absolutely really worth of gods love, you then are simply worth of a loving motion, then you may also deliver a loving motion sincerely to provide it. And this is the important thing to peace. All souls are identical no matter their variations. You can see why it's dangerous to be irritated.

Chapter 7: How To Tell If Your Memory Is Real

1. A past life memory isn't always a mere reminiscence but an energetic recording of an event you absolutely expert somewhere inside the past. This is not such as you forgetting to feed your cat. It's an emotion and an occasion. When it comes for your ground, it is a very strong "sincere" knowledge which you were there earlier than. Your mind cannot make this up!

2. Your reminiscences might be very specific and FEEL familiar and like you KNOW you were there. You can't duplicate this shape of feeling. You're actually seeing your soul's travels from from one Era to the subsequent. You've lived, completed that life, crossed over after which determined on a trendy existence to get to this 2d in time.

three. The reminiscences you may have will NOT resemble a play, film, or cultural event you have got ever seen. And you may even take into account a demanding reminiscence that you can by no means replica on your very own. So there must be a motive you're recalling a reminiscence.

4. You'll be interested in someone so strongly, you could simply need to allow the connection to seem so you can see why you have got been drawn together. Though, many individuals who are given the opportunity to examine some factor generally have a tendency to recognize it quite speedy.

5. If your reminiscence surfaces in a dream, it will be very specific and you will commonly bear in mind it in high-quality detail at the same time as you wake. And because it's like saved statistics, you need to be able to maintain in thoughts it prolonged when you're aware.

6. Unless you have got a own family records of highbrow infection this is associated with hallucinationd for numerous motives, you could now not start to

hallucinate. A hallucination feels empty and acquired't have a robust feeling of familiarity to it like a reminiscence will. If you endure in thoughts a beyond lifestyles, write it down and ask your self why you think you may make it up?

7. Many arm chair logicians have tried to dismiss the recollection of beyond lives with the precept that we want to virtually be experiencing a magnetic, weather primarily based however exceptional clinical phenomenon that would create a hallucination.

But permit me guarantee you that there may be no such hassle as a "top notch natural solar blast polar shift magnetic hyperbolic occurrence" or some different fictitious occasion that would create a functionality for a hallucination. If this turned into true, we'd all have a essential trouble even as working, using or trying to feature normally. The rationalization seems so severe, I ought to ask what is so worrying approximately the priority to need to present an explanation for it away.

To repeat, our memories exist energetically interior your frame, moderate frame, and interest. They are particular to you and can not virtually be fabricated. And they can't change and provide you with a unique finishing or characters. The reminiscence will always be the equal. A hallucination does not have any direction.

Chapter 8: Reasons You Can't Remember

1. Your first lifestyles ever.

2. Buried lifestyles which could had been demanding or that is blocked.

3. Is that you are in the procedure of a specific lesson that you should stay centered on. Or the memory might not help this lesson.

four. You also can need to perform a touch meditation and self healing to open your thoughts.

HOW TO TELL WHEN YOU ARE REACTING TO A PAST LIFE

MEMORY BEFORE YOU CAN FULLY RECALL IT

Keep in mind that a few memories will no longer in fact floor in extremely good visible detail however you WILL locate yourself responding to the person within the the front of you as in case you truly left off from the final moment you lived with them. Not from your reminiscence subconsciously as it's no longer excellent a reminiscence, but it is in that you left off with this soul you're experiencing with.

Ex. You keep calling your cousin your uncle. It's this subconscious element you do. You do not recognize why.

You continually tour by way of the use of educate regardless of what regardless of the truth that planes or boats might be faster. You in fact love trains.

You continuously loved a country and you continually loved a fine town. You continually favored to move there and no character ever recommended you about it.

You have continually had a talents for playing a specific tool. You definitely never wanted education or only some and you bought it.

The key proper right here is that you FEEL your capability like you've got commonly been able to do it! You KNOW you have got constantly been this individual or you've got been together earlier than.

As you decide through your skills and relationships, you may clearly and step by step take into account the lives you lived while you first discovered this ability or bonded with this soul.

IMPORTANT POINTS TO PONDER

Never pressure a memory to floor. Always experience it out. Ask your self what you need to realise from this memory? And deliver thanks at the same time as you can endure in thoughts or gain a message from your soul.

Never strain a worrying memory to floor. You want this to be slight and maintain carefully.

If you could see your air of mystery or your soul energetically you may be amazed and inspired! It can without a doubt extend outward from your physical body by means of the usage of way of numerous feet and it carries pretty some information about your beyond lifestyles reviews.

It can experience like a vibration looking for to fill your head. It can enjoy like pressure searching out to push upwards. It can enjoy like a woosh from your feet upwards. This is all electricity. This is a tangible sensation that can not be imagined or hallucinated. You cannot make it up!

Another manner is through a deep facts or an urge to tell a person a message.

The first a part of in reality recalling your beyond lives is which you want to revel in and permit it to surface. Every motion, the entirety that you do is as strongly related to your feelings. Your subconscious records every element and each crucial element whether or no longer you understand that that's what it's far doing or not.

Pay hobby to the manner you revel in about positive people and conditions. I actually have worked with human beings that without delay set me off or worried me and I did now not apprehend why but I need to pay interest my inner self speaking and I knew that is what it become.

A manager without delay made me revel in unhappy, and involved. I did not recognize why however in my thoughts I should see her sporting a nun's dependancy. After a while, I become able to don't forget that she ran an orphanage and he or she or he turned into very strict. She modified into a totally tough boss in this existence and I was a small infant that have been brought to her. There changed into an imbalance and I come to be given the possibility to reset it. She emerge as a bully in this lifestyles and we needed to paintings together without a revel in of ownership.

WHAT HAPPENS IF YOU CAN'T REMEMBER THE LIFE BUT

YOU KNOW YOU'RE FEELING IT.

Some lives you are only solving the imbalance among you and each different and also you do not want to recognize what the life have become. Just enjoy. This method you can not see it. What to do in a case like this:

Ask your self:

1. Where does your heart allow you to recognize to move?

2. Is this relationship healthy for me?

3. Do they have got my top notch pursuits at coronary heart?

4. Do I actually have theirs?

five. What is it that I'm intended to be to this man or woman?

6. Who am I to this person?

You can in most instances, with enough time to think about your courting, parent out in which the imbalance is.

Again, everything is active. Everything! It's not handiest a memory which you're pulling up. It's a reminiscence that is connected to power linked to emotion. You're in essence attempting to drag up information from a few minutes ago in the life of your soul. Like a recording of time to your being.

Your subconscious is recalling in advance than the "dream" or reminiscence itself is surfacing. And inwardly your inner map of the life you created is continually at paintings. Whether you comprehend it or no longer.

So from time to time you are gonna have a reminiscence this is working with you however you are not gonna be capable of take into account it and also you are not gonna apprehend why you experience the manner that you do approximately some component. For instance you have got a chum which you speak to as speedy as a while and you have not any idea why but you absolutely love them unconditionally. They're form of a jerk but you will do a little detail for them. Then you've got were given a round the corner neighbor who in no manner did something to you in my view however you hate them with a Passion and you do no longer comprehend why.

We are installation conditions at some point of our lives to create new karma, appropriate karma, repair horrible karma and examine schooling. We come once more to learn how to pick our battles, a way to have a look at numerous virtues and in essence, the way to expand our souls. We come once more to justify troubles that had been created for a few past lives. We come returned to make new friends and to start new analyzing cycles over again. So people from our past lives are going to be set up positions or in locations with us in order that we're capable of observe from them or healing what we broke, if some factor. Period.

Therefore you want to be aware of your emotional connections to people. This is fundamental to facts a past existence reminiscence that you could not be able to completely bear in thoughts but it's miles in fact surfacing subconsciously.

This is natural and it takes place all of the time even whilst you don't even comprehend it. We are spiritual beings. Every single human on Earth is a non secular being with a soul. So maximum folks have already lived more than one lives. It is feasible to haven't any recollections because of the reality this will be your first lifestyles on this planet. If you've got were given ordinary recollections that seem to make no enjoy, it is mainly viable which you as soon as lived on some other planet. Don't choose a reminiscence at the identical time as you dream it or even because it surfaces.

There is a distinction among divine love and romantic love. Just because you've got got been no longer rescued from a trouble the manner you accept as true with you studied you have got been purported to be might not advise you have been now not shown a manner to rescue yourself. The divine thoughts and coronary coronary heart is just like God.

Let's talk about the stigma. Why perform a touch people overthink whilst you talk the exceeded existence recollections you percentage with them and others are great?

WHAT'S WEIRD ABOUT IT?

Nothing is weird about taking walks approximately reincarnation. But human beings do will be predisposed to react to any trouble rely they do not need warfare of phrases from or to relive pain and suffering. And every body maintain pain and suffering from preceding lives to a point in our souls. For the ones motives, a few people have a tendency to keep away from the conversation. The following are a few reasons that I even have discovered over time:

1. Signs of a tumultuous courting in a beyond life. You had your coronary coronary heart broken or out of area a loved one.

2. A relative or authority decide used a tough rule from a religious group to educate and demand they do now not ever communicate about something angers God. Ex. "Devil's paintings"

3. They do NOT like discussing emotions.

four. They have an overzealous need to be on pinnacle of factors with the truth they had been raised with. They do not want to be out of manipulate or be incorrect.

In fact, anyone have them and anyone revel in them even if we're capable of't actually consider them. We are here to research and we deliver the ones memories with us everywhere. We all study a inner steering to get us through lifestyles that is in part fixing some aspect hurtful we professional previously.

The reality is internal you. Always. I definitely have observed that if you can take into account something that desires to be healed and the individual that introduced on it in a beyond life is your state of affairs, they may commonly near up and no longer allow you pass any in addition and on occasion close you down and attempt to stroll away from you. This is widely speaking due to the fact they're coronary coronary coronary heart is really not ready to admit or get hold of the facts you have were given have been given for them. But if you could recollect this, then you definately don't need them to heal always. They do not need to admit something. This 2nd may be which will widely recognized that you are "OK" and that you made it through your closing lifestyles and into this one and your soul remains intact and that it's true enough to forgive and walk a long way from this. Never count on a whole apology from a person that harm you in a beyond lifestyles unless they may be additionally on their direction to a spiritual awakening. Understand in that you're for your very own soul growth with this person and skip beforehand.

Chapter 9: How Does All This Help You With Your Awakening?

First allow's outline awakening. This is in reality at the equal time as you learn how to clearly well known your private soul and your connection to the universe. There is not any rule about how speedy or slowly this have to occur. But your awakening can rise up in a single lifestyles or over the span of many!

Just like whilst the soul is perfecting and getting again to its knowledge of the slight, your awakening does now not need to stand up right now.

The maximum important a part of experiencing your awakening is the growth of your mind, coronary coronary heart, and soul simultaneously. We have a propensity to art work on our intelligence first and search for answers in advance than know-how the actual which means that love but we want love definitely as an awful lot.

Understanding love is our key to expertise the universe and what makes it tick.

You can spend your life meditation for solutions, but without compassion you continue to satisfactory learn how to a few element and no longer a manner to like and don't forget it.

We are all souls on a adventure. Every artist, custodian, mom, father, villain, infant, teacher, scholar, road rage reason pressure, enterprise enterprise owner, criminal, policeman, criminal professional, flesh presser, retiree, cat, dog, horse and ect. We all select to incarnate for a completely unique reason and this is to locate and understand the know-how and love awaiting us to align with it. How you choose to gain this is your preference.

Hopefully thru this e book you have were given determined the number one steps to start your adventure to cognizance and spirit's awakening. Remember that this can take numerous years to even lives so do not give up!

One greater lesson you examine on your manner to enlightenment, is that in case your soul is real and you're getting to know instructions and re-aligning with the reality this is our supply, then so is every person else one step at a time, one lifestyles at a time. You observe we're all in the identical boat, and all have the same struggles and all this is on the earth is temporary. We are all running collectively to achieve our maximum selves.

Chapter 10: Prompts To Help Jog Your Memory

In this phase, use the questions underneath that will help you consider the recollections that you'd need to release and undergo in mind. These are designed to help you sense out your connections to circle of relatives, friends, co-people. Take a while with these and if you don't experience like writing then down, then take one question and contemplate it. Try now not to overthink it and alternatively deliver it time. If the query doesn't assist, then strive some different one.

Know that except you're residing your first actual lifestyles, you surely could have beyond life reminiscences buried in your soul. The different cause you gained't consider a beyond lifestyles is if you are not intended to as it acquired't serve your reason presently in your lifestyles. As I noted formerly, in no manner strain it, or attempt too hard to don't forget. If you've got any reminiscences, they'll ground absolutely and it's always high-quality to place the maximum moderate intentions within the again of your efforts.

As you begin, ask your better self to thrill assist you allow any memories a very good manner to serve you currently as gently as possible. And supply thank you at the same time as you do. And you may need to duplicate it.

You should ask for specifics and be as extraordinary as possible. You can do that in a journal or via remaining your eyes and focussing at the aspect of your aim in your better self.

1. What is the dominant emotion you experience in any conflicts you have got with a member of the family? If you fight or argue frequently, how does it give up end result? Do you land up having to define your self or do you walk aware exhausted?

2. What is the handiest issue approximately every argument that stands proud the most to you? Power war? Do they lack apprehend or compassion after they want some aspect from you?

3. What style of get dressed do you feel or see to your thoughts that you could have worn even as you first professional the emotion?

four. What mode of transportation are you capable of consider the use of?

five. What age involves thoughts?

6. Have you ever met each person that stood out to you or pulled your interest in an unforgettable way? You may not even communicate to them any greater and also you in no way forgot them?

7. Do you understand all of us that makes you sense anxious for no motive? You get traumatic for no certainly particular purpose in any respect? You can barely

communicate round them, however but you commonly are notable and don't go through any social anxiety?

8. Have you ever met each person that you get collectively with proper now and like you will be awesome buddies or siblings?

nine. Have you ever met everybody, or apprehend every person that you keep looking to name your dad, brother, mom, grandma, son or daughter who is not this relation?

Take every of these and definitely suppose on them. These questions are not any great from in case your had simply met these humans or had a present day conversation with them, however in fact, you probably did. It truly happened to be severa years in the beyond.

If your emotions are surfacing as you undergo the ones? Do you get at the aspect of the humans you revel in? Why do you observed you do? Why do you trust you studied you do?

10. Have you ever suffered from any form of tension at the equal time as using later in lifestyles? Or any kind bizarre contamination that clinical docs cannot make experience of?

11. Do you get emotional for the duration of activities just like the Trumpet Solo "Taps" or any track associated with a first-rate ancient event that you recognise you probably did no longer take part in, on this lifestyles?

12. Do you've got had been given an irrational worry of flying, being in water, on a deliver, or in small locations?

thirteen. Do you have got an urge to eat more than you need to despite the fact that topics aren't demanding?

14. Do you have got were given have been given an urge to be overly cautious

even at the same time as you're aware of it's now not critical to gain this?

15. Are you drawn to certain factors of conflict, the clothes in Edwardian or Victorian eras, tanks, old style vehicles or feel comfortable round horses, horse and buggies?

16. Birthmarks and snap shots:

I in no way use an antique picture to determine how I regarded in a past life, and I in no way pass thru the usage of birthmarks. I continually bypass through what I'm interested by and the manner I experience approximately it. This does NOT mean that a birthmark can't be evidence from a beyond existence, however it would want to be a completely specific original mark in a specific place and you will ought to revel in like you recognize how to procure it. There is probably some form of memory you could even barely undergo in thoughts.

This being said, if you have each or each of these gadgets, deliver your self time to revel in it out and be conscious in case you honestly can experience a familiarity with this. It's too smooth to really assume that your birthmark is a whole indication that it become from a past existence. We all have them and all of us have a number of them and we really can not determine if it manner anything with out being capable of experience it. A proper past lifestyles memory will revel in such as you realise in which it came from.

As you undergo the listing, ask your self what you apprehend about every object. Your internal voice will usually let you comprehend at once and you could have an urge do some thing a particular way.

Years in the past I become getting a few aspect at paintings and I have come to be on the brink of leave and I had simply met someone that I wasn't sure If i used to be friends with but or not. They had been far off and regarded to no longer make certain what they wished from me. I bear in mind as I modified into deliberating them, "Well, inside the occasion that they want to speak to me they may. And this time, I received't allow myself to assume shortage. I will attempt to suppose more abundantly."

Because I had this skills considering young humans, I turn out to be quick capable of hold in thoughts that in a preceding life I grow to be so involved approximately survival I didn't realise that had the functionality to assist myself. I knew I become wondering very restricted thoughts in that existence! The emotions surfaced earlier than the memory did! I couldn't absolutely keep in mind that life but, however I knew that I have become financially strapped and my first mistake changed into to anticipate that I modified into commonly going to be broke or in want of coins.

I quickly recalled that existence in whole element and knew that this grow to be no longer going to be an smooth friendship due to the truth I had made the karma with this soul from being horrible. In addition to this, I observed out that they've been now not as articulate with terms as I became in this existence and just so they had been no longer approximately to talk up and start a communication with me. I would possibly ought to be the one to mention a few element after which as soon as I tried to, it didn't depend to them. This is the lesson I determined out about carefully drawing close to others that might not share my abilities. I stated this in advance within the ebook.

Back to helping you endure in mind, it's vital to apprehend that if you have lived past lives and feature any reminiscences that might let you heal from past trauma, the ones memories are surely saved and buried for your slight frame. They will arise as favored and you'll experience them for your intuition. The magic isn't for your reminiscence banks, it's within the manner your body, mind and soul art work together to maintain all the expertise you gain from each existence. In essence, the actual magic is on the identical time as you recognise which you have a soul that is privy to. And when you apprehend you have got were given a soul and that you have lived and you come back to the realization that you're countless and you've got got lived already to your very personal, then you genuinely start to enjoy your spiritual awakening! Give it time and it's going to appear for you!

Chapter 11: How To Know You Experiencing A Spiritual Awakening

This isn't a shocking massive awakening earlier moment. This takes time or maybe lives to experience. And it's critical which you apprehend that definitely because of the reality you have were given an interest of your soul, does NOT advise that you understand endless compassion, countless cognizance, and unconditional love. Your get right of entry to to the universe takes all three! You can be an aware soul but even though no longer apprehend why all souls want to get the hazard to move over and circulate into the mild, even though their criminals or unstable human beings. The below is a tick list of things you can experience as you turn out to be greater privy to your soul.

1. You can see the bigger image in the whole thing.

2. Your vibration becomes more potent.

3.   You can preserve near how a love so powerful exists in a universe with so much pain and suffering.

four. You can understand why even terrible humans can pass returned to the slight for recovery as opposed to judgment.

five.   You apprehend on the identical time as judgment is truely essential (to maintain your existence) and while it's not.

6.   You're an awful lot a whole lot less afraid to face unresolved problems.

7.   You start to permit pass of antique patterns or toxic notion structures.

8.   You may be extra on my own, or like no person is aware of you because of the fact others seem greater near minded.

9.   You will start to apprehend people who assume in any other case from you.

10.   You can revel in panic assaults, but this is because of the reality the ego is used

to protective you and attempting to influence you a protracted way from hazard. If you're stepping into a latest section in your existence and your trying a few thing new, you may enjoy worried or panicky about this.

eleven. You might also lose a few friends as your belief system adjustments or shifts, but if your friends aren't inquisitive about your mind and end up lousy, then this can be a sign that this dating is finished for now and you can should go away them to assume for themselves and select out what works for them.

12. Anything in life that requires trade will cause stress and tension. Your ego will conflict together in conjunction with your modifications for a minute, but you may discern it out.

Spiritual awakening happens to anybody finally. The key's to try to ensure to live genuinely sincere with yourself and permit your self to make errors. You WILL misunderstand your guidance and instinct at instances and you may get an ego at times while you need to be humble.

Just consider that the moderate you're searching for to align with is a far big model of your better self. The moderate is know-how, reality, love, know-how, staying power and divine intelligence and prefer all one-of-a-kind souls on Earth, it's a divine proper. We are all same and are all at the course, regardless of the truth that we each select to are looking for it in our way and our very personal time.

Chapter 12: The Intriguing Concept Of Past Lives

Have you ever had that unusual feeling of getting lived fine memories in advance than, no matter the reality that you are exceptional it's miles the number one time you have ever lived them? Have you skilled that feeling of familiarity with places you've got were given in no manner visited, or felt an inexplicable connection to sure eras in statistics?

If so, welcome to the world of the mysterious, of the enigma of past lives. This idea, in its most simple form, holds that souls are eternal and stay multiple lives all through the eons, each of which shapes us and contributes to the evolution of our popularity. Why is this applicable, you ask? Let me allow you to recognize that this idea has the electricity to transform our facts of ourselves, our relationships and our lifestyles in popular.

So what clearly are past lives? In its most primary form, past lives are the precept or notion that an character soul lives many lives in fantastic time intervals and in incredible our our bodies. Although this idea can also appear unusual to some, it's far a commonplace belief in lots of cultures and spiritual traditions spherical the arena. In fact, some of the region's oldest philosophies, along side Hinduism and Buddhism, have held for plenty of years that our souls are everlasting and go through cycles of start, demise and rebirth on their manner to enlightenment.

But how can this historic concept healthful into our modern expertise of the arena? How can a spiritual idea coexist with our know-how of technological understanding and psychology?

This is in which the idea of past lives will become sincerely captivating. For it is not truly an unsubstantiated mystical perception. There is a growing empirical evidence base that indicates that past life regression may have actual, tangible rate in our every day lives. It can offer us with a broader mindset on who we are, help us recognize and triumph over unexplained traumas and fears, or maybe form our identification and relationships in massive techniques.

But in advance than we delve into that proof and what it is able to do for us, it's miles important to understand why beyond lives exist. Why, you ask, could our soul choose to undergo this cycle of existence after lifestyles? Wouldn't it be less hard, greater snug, to live handiest as soon as, take a look at what there's to analyze, and then relaxation for all time in eternity?

The method to that question, my costly reader, can be decided in the ancient idea of soul increase. According to this angle, every lifestyles we stay is an possibility to take a look at and growth, to enjoy the sector from a one of a kind attitude, to cope with unique disturbing situations and schooling. Like an actor who takes on many in reality considered one of a type roles throughout his career to increase and satisfactory his craft, our soul chooses a variety of lifetimes to boom new abilities, benefit knowledge and evolve right proper into a higher form of awareness.

This concept of soul growth is contemplated within the terms of psychotherapist and pioneer of past lifestyles regression remedy, Dr. Brian Weiss. In his e book "Many Lives, Many Masters" (1988), Weiss recounts his experience with a affected person who, underneath hypnosis, started to take into account her beyond lives. What she decided at some stage in the ones sessions no longer only changed her know-how of her very very very own lifestyles, but also her view of psychotherapy. Weiss wrote: "Through Catherine (his affected man or woman), I found out that our lives are everlasting, that the soul is immortal, and that we're a super deal greater than bodily our bodies limited via place and time."

So how are we able to start to find out our very very own beyond lives? Is this a few thing first-class psychics or expert therapists can do? Or is it a adventure we're able to all embark on?

This is in which the intrigue intensifies. While past life regressions are frequently accomplished in a healing placing, there also are strategies we are able to start to discover our non-public beyond lives on our non-public. Therapist Ann C. Barham, in her e-book The Past Life Perspective (2016), offers us lots of strategies and practices, which includes meditation, hypnosis and dream interpretation, that we can use to delve into the depths of our past lives.

But what in case you though discover it difficult to simply accept as proper with in the concept of beyond lives? What in case you discover all of it too weird, too esoteric?

Don't worry, you are not by myself in that feeling. There are many those who feel the equal way. And that is wherein generation is available in.

Psychologist Dr. Ian Stevenson committed quite a few his career to coming across instances of children spontaneously recalling their past lives. In his ebook Twenty Cases Suggestive of Reincarnation (1966), he documented a sequence of instances in which youngsters supplied accurate and verifiable information about lives they seemed to have lived in advance than. Although those times aren't "proof" of reincarnation within the traditional medical experience, they do offer fascinating evidence supporting the existence of past lives.

Wait a minute, am I saying you want to believe in reincarnation now? Not precisely. My motive, like many on this situation, isn't always to steer you of anything, but rather to provide you a cutting-edge lens thru which you can have a have a look at your very very own life. Because on the give up of the day, perception in beyond lives, like a few different belief, is a private choice.

What I advise to you is that this: What in case you undergo in mind the possibility of beyond lives now not as an unquestionable fact, however as a tool, a manner to growth your expertise of your self and the arena? What in case you attempt to maintain an open mind and permit your self to be guided by using the usage of the use of interest and intrigue?

Let me illustrate this with a sensible example, imagining a beyond lifestyles. Have you ever professional a strong enchantment to a particular tradition or generation? Let's say, as an instance, that you have usually been inquisitive about historic Egypt. The pyramids, the pharaohs, the perception in existence after dying, the whole lot is seemingly familiar and appealing to you.

Now, believe that you have the opportunity to find out the possibility that your soul may additionally moreover have lived a life in that element and area. Imagine that, via meditation or hypnosis, you could unencumber reminiscences of a past existence as a scribe in ancient Egypt, documenting the greatness of the pharaohs and taking detail within the mysterious rituals of the afterlife.

How may that trade your angle of your self? How wouldn't it now not no longer affect you to discover that you had been as soon as a part of a subculture that has constantly involved you? It can also need to offer an reason on your appeal to ancient Egypt, however past that, it may also give you a brand new information of who you're on a soul stage.

You can be thinking, is there any concrete evidence of such an revel in? You is probably amazed to research that there are various debts of human beings who have had very similar reviews. Take the instance of famend creator and mystic Ruth Bernard Law Montgomery, who in her ebook "Companions Along the Way" (1974), describes how beyond life regression durations led her to bear in mind lives as a lousy peasant in medieval England, a sailor on a Viking supply, and a disciple of Jesus.

Through the ones research, Bernard Law Bernard Law Montgomery advanced a deeper understanding of her cause in life and a profound empathy for humans from all walks of lifestyles. In her case, beyond existence exploration have turn out to be a precious device for self-know-how and non secular evolution.

So, how about embarking on this journey into the unknown? Are you inclined to open the door of your mind and find out the infinite possibilities of your soul?

Of path, there is continuously the threat that you may come upon painful or annoying memories from beyond lives. After all, no longer all of our lives won't had been glad or smooth. But even those tough reminiscences can be treasured, as they permit us to face and overcome vintage traumas that can be affecting our modern lives in strategies we do no longer even recognize.

Psychiatrist and writer of the e-book "Life Before Life" (2005), Dr. Helen Wambach, executed large research on beyond lifestyles regressions. She located that many humans have been capable of address and solve beyond existence traumas through these opinions, resulting in large development in their emotional and physical nicely-being.

Of path, past life exploration is not for all and sundry. It calls for braveness, openness and a willingness to challenge into the unknown. However, for folks that are inclined to take on the mission, the rewards may be profoundly transformative.

What if this e-book might be your key to free up the doorways of time and find out the infinite lives your soul should have lived? What secrets and techniques and techniques and techniques may also additionally want to you find out? What fears should you face and overcome? What training should you examine?

The famous psychologist Carl Jung, whose "Memories, Dreams, Thoughts" (1962) laid a number of the principles for our modern know-how of the psyche, believed that every person deliver with us the imprints of beyond lives in what he known as the collective unconscious. Through the exploration of those imprints, Jung cautioned, we are capable of loose up a greater records of ourselves and our place within the global.

In essence, the thrilling concept of beyond lives worrying conditions us to increase our notion of what is viable, to impeach our maximum clean assumptions about life, loss of existence and identity, and to discover the hidden depths of our very personal psyche.

You have released right into a fascinating journey, my steeply-priced reader. Throughout this ebook, I will guide you through the complex spheres of time and area, piercing the veils of oblivion, to discover the strains your soul has left in its direction.

Together, we're capable of discover the clocks of the soul, our spiritual timeline, inside the next bankruptcy. We'll delve into how our souls, via a couple of existences, may have woven a complex internet of recollections, instructions and relationships. I'll show you strategies, thru analyzing those spiritual timelines, we're capable of gain fascinating insights into who we simply are at the soul level.

So, are you prepared to preserve on this thrilling and transformative journey? Are you equipped to preserve exploring the reflect of time, to face yourself in its reflections and to find out what your beyond lives have to expose to you?

I promise it will probably be a journey entire of surprises, discoveries and, particularly, extra self-expertise. So, whilst you are equipped, take a deep breath, open your thoughts and coronary coronary heart, and flip the page. Your soul awaits you on the other aspect. Until the following chapter, my pal.

Chapter 13: The Soul Clocks

Ah, time! Isn't it fascinating, costly reader, how we regularly think about time as a at once line? A route that takes us from a issue inside the beyond thru the existing and into the future. But what if I counseled you that this angle is really too restricted? What if I told you that the proper nature of time is lots extra complex, a good deal more cute and multidimensional?

Welcome, soul adventurer, to the location of soul clocks!

The "spiritual timeline," as it might be known as, is extra like a spiral than a at once line. Imagine a snail shell. The manner it unfolds, from a critical point outward in an ever-widening spiral pattern. That's a extra accurate metaphor for the manner our souls experience time. And in each curve of this spiral is a existence we've got lived. Each is a segment of the spiral, an critical factor of the soul's trajectory.

Do you find out it intriguing and enjoy ready to find out this multidimensional thoughts-set of life? I guarantee you that, within the next few pages, your mind will boom and your heart will throb with a contemporary know-how of the wondrous complexity of your very very personal being.

The British philosopher and mathematician Alfred North Whitehead, in his art work "Process and Reality" (1929), expounded the idea that reality is not static, however is a way of turning into. Is that no longer precisely what we're experiencing in our lives, a ordinary becoming? Every day, each hour, every right away is a step in our soul's adventure. And if we need to understand that this journey isn't always confined to a unmarried existence, but encompasses numerous existences, how might probably that exchange our angle of the location and of ourselves?

Transpersonal psychologist Stanislav Grof, in his influential paintings "Realms of the

Human Unconscious: Observations from LSD Research" (1975), described stories of topics who regarded to bear in thoughts or relive activities from what regarded to be past lives. If the ones debts are real, it suggests an information of recognition and time that departs from conventional notions. It demanding situations us to endure in mind the opportunity that our souls, over a couple of lifetimes, have been on a journey of increase and mastering.

Now, high priced reader, let us pause proper right here for a 2d. I would like you to imagine your self on the middle of that spiral, at the problem in which all paths converge. As we flow into the following sections of this financial catastrophe, accept as actual with that you are exploring this spiral, each twist, every turn, every curve, every revolution. Each turn of the spiral is a step for your journey into the deeper expertise of your religious self.

Now, as we pass deeper into this exploration, it's far essential to cognizance on the artwork of some key thinkers in the task of psychology and philosophy. Swiss psychiatrist Carl Jung, acknowledged for his research on the human psyche and the unconscious, proposed in his works which incorporates "Archetypes and the Collective Unconscious" (1959) the concept that everybody percentage a large sea of common stories and logos that move beyond our man or woman lives. Doesn't this appear to offer a basis for the perception of beyond lives and a soul that travels thru time?

As we maintain our journey down the spiral of time, we can also recollect the contribution of modern authors together with Brian Weiss, a psychiatrist who has come to be a key determine inside the location of past-life regression treatment. In his ebook "Many Lives, Many Masters" (1988), Weiss recounts his experience going for walks with sufferers who, under hypnosis, recalled stories that appeared to return back from beyond lives. These recollections, often associated with deep traumas, regarded to play a role within the sufferers' present troubles, and via way of confronting and knowledge these memories, many decided more peace and know-how in their present lives.

This brings us to an important query which you might be asking yourself proper now. How can we get entry to these past lives and people deep-seated critiques within the soul? Well, perhaps the answer is nearer than you observed. Have you ever had a feel of déjà vu, a revel in of familiarity with a place, man or woman or occasion which you can't offer an reason of? Or perhaps you have had colourful desires that appear greater actual than fact itself, taking you to places and instances you've got never professional to your present day life?

So, pricey reader, as we keep to move in advance on our journey, I need to invite you to open yourself to the possibility that those studies can be glimpses of your past lives. Some can also moreover brush aside those studies as mere illusions or figments of the creativeness, but I ask you, my friend, to maintain an open thoughts. For who's aware about what secrets of the soul we would find out if we allow ourselves to discover past what we typically bear in thoughts possible?

To illustrate greater vividly the thoughts we have been discussing, permit us to delve into the account of 1 in every of Brian Weiss's regression training. His affected person, whom he calls Catherine in his ebook, became a girl plagued with the useful resource of phobias and panic assaults. Under hypnosis, Catherine commenced to take into account living in a unique body, in a special time and location.

There have come to be something precise about the unique description of his past lifestyles. It become now not a vague tale, but a chain of lived, sensory activities. The information she provided, from the clothes she wore to the residence she lived in, were too precise and coherent to be just imaginary. But beyond the story itself, what become in reality transformative have become how Catherine became capable of hyperlink the traumas of that beyond existence in conjunction with her modern fears.

So I ask you, high priced reader, have you ever ever experienced an irrational worry or unexplained phobia? Could or no longer it is that this fear is rooted in a beyond existence trauma, prepared to be determined, confronted and healed?

This is a essential element in information the idea of our non secular timelines. They aren't actually beyond life tales; they will be reports that resonate in our cutting-edge lives, affecting the manner we assume, sense and behave. Therefore, the journey inside the path of coming across and understanding our beyond lives is not excellent a curious exploration, but a powerful device for recovery and self-facts.

This brings us to the door of the attention of the first-rate spiritual masters of the East. The Dalai Lama, in his ebook "The Universe in a Single Atom" (2005), advocates a fusion of technology and spirituality to get to the lowest of the mysteries of the universe and of ourselves. And what more thriller is there than the individual of our very very very own life, which seems to growth beyond the boundaries of time and area?

As my expensive buddy, our journey collectively is clearly starting. We have mapped out the contours of our journey, and now we're prepared to move deeper into the sector of past lives and soul timelines. With each step we take collectively, I preference you revel in increasingly the pride of this top notch exploration. Are you geared up to maintain, my pal?

We walk this path of discovery collectively, expensive reader, and we are already starting to see how our past life reminiscences must have a right away impact on our gift life. Like Catherine, we might also moreover deliver with us wounds from the beyond that also need to be healed. But additionally, like Catherine, we've got the capability to face the ones fears and traumas, and sooner or later loose ourselves from them. This is the promise that lies on the coronary heart of our exploration of soul timelines.

Of direction, we want to moreover address the traumatic situations inherent in beyond-existence regression. As Carl Sagan as it must be stated in "The World and Its Demons" (1995), "fantastic affirmation requires super proof." And at the identical time as beyond-life regression may be powerfully transformative on a private degree, it additionally offers tough questions that need to be approached with rigor and openness.

Let me assure you, my buddy, that the ones questions can be the hassle of our subsequent conversation. In the chapters to come back lower again, we are able to look at encounters with echoes from our beyond lives, have a examine the scientific proof, and don't forget historic and cutting-edge bills that shed mild in this phenomenon.

Yes, there are traumatic conditions along the way. But as any suitable vacationer is aware of, worrying situations are exactly what make excursion interesting. They invite us to develop, to examine, to impeach and to deepen our understanding.

So a protracted way, we've got explored together the fascinating possibilities offered via the concept of past lives and have all started out out to get to the lowest of the threads of our non secular timelines. Now, I invite you to look at together with me as we delve even deeper into this fascinating journey. Are you prepared to take the following step?

The adventure ahead guarantees to be interesting, hard and transformative. Together, we are capable of solve the mysteries of our past lives, find out how they intertwine with our modern-day lives, and find out how we are able to use this realize-how to heal, develop and thrive. Because at the stop of the day, the purpose of this journey is to discover the attention and peace we all are searching out. Are you geared up, my pal, to embark on the next level of our journey together? Onward, the course awaits!

Chapter 14: Echo Encounters

Not all encounters are physical, nor are all interactions on a tangible plane. There are opinions that arise in the landscapes of our minds, in the sensitive vicinity among sleep and wakefulness, in flashes of intuition that appear at the most unexpected moments. It is the ones encounters with "echoes" from our beyond lives that we are able to find out in this bankruptcy. And on the equal time as you can question yourself, my buddy, whether the ones reports are actual or in reality fantasies, I invite you to open your mind to the possibility that our fact and our identity are an extended way extra complex and enriching than we ever imagined.

Why is that this difficulty depend crucial? Because the ones encounters with past-existence echoes can provide us with particular and precious insights approximately ourselves. They can assist us apprehend our routine varieties of conduct, our affinities and aversions, or even our life desires and features.

The idea of having visions or intuitions of beyond lives may additionally moreover moreover appear mysterious, even incomprehensible. But for those who've skilled those manifestations, they will be very actual and often deeply tremendous. And at the equal time as the ones echoes of past lives can gift themselves in lots of strategies, they often come in the form of visions, desires and intuitive feelings.

Let me ask you, my buddy, have you ever ever ever ever had a deja vu so intense that it appeared along with you've got been remembering an revel in you in no way had on this lifetime? Or in all likelihood a dream so outstanding and sensible that it left you thinking if it was a reminiscence in preference to actually a creation of your thoughts? These are genuinely a number of the techniques wherein our beyond life echoes can show up.

And at the same time as the concept of getting visions or intuitions of beyond lives may be disconcerting inside the beginning, don't forget the terms of Carl Jung in "Memories, Dreams, Reflections" (1962): "In each oldsters there may be a few specific whom we do no longer understand. He speaks to us in goals and informs us of our hidden longings." Could or not it is that those 'others' to whom Jung refers are certainly ourselves in our past lives?

As we are able to see in this financial disaster, beyond-life visions and intuitions can act as a window thru which we will look at our souls and take a look at the threads that bind our existences collectively through the years. Through the ones domestic home home windows, we are able to start to higher understand who we really are, and how our past reviews have everyday our gift existence.

Of direction, not definitely anyone agrees with this concept. As we're capable of see in

Chapter 18, there are criticisms and worrying situations to past-existence regression. But for now, I invite you to set aside your prejudices and open yourself to the opportunity. After all, isn't it hobby and open-mindedness that make us real explorers of the mystery that is lifestyles itself?

In reality, as we dive into the mysteries of past lives, we will see that this concept is neither new nor radical. Throughout statistics, severa cultures and philosophies have first rate the concept of reincarnation and past lives as an vital a part of their worldview.

For instance, in his ebook "The Lives of the Masters" (1986), the non secular writer Baird T. Spalding recounts the travels of a studies institution in the Himalayas, wherein they met Ascended Masters who spoke to them approximately their beyond lives and confirmed them how those past opinions affected their gift lives. Similarly, the thirteenth century philosopher and mystic, Mevlana Jalaluddin Rumi, as speedy as said, "I die as a mineral and emerge as a plant, I die as a plant and rise as an animal, I die as an animal and end up a person. Why need to I fear? When did I become much less thru loss of existence?" (Masnavi, book 3, 3901-3903). These historic thoughts permit us to recognize that the idea of reincarnation and past lives isn't a peripheral notion, but an important a part of human spirituality within the direction of the centuries.

Of direction, not all beyond-life echoes are transcendent or maybe easy to recognize. Sometimes, they may be as mundane as a sense of familiarity at the same time as touring a place for the number one time, or an unexplained taste for a particular manner of lifestyles or ancient technology. In "The Search for the Past" (1988), psychologist and author Brian Weiss recounts how his sufferers skilled beyond-life reminiscences inside the course of regression remedy periods, some of which have been trivial or perhaps comical, collectively with a memory of being a bored farmer in the Middle Ages.

These encounters with echoes of beyond lives can arouse a sizeable style of emotions, from confusion to fascination, from skepticism to faith. But what topics isn't a lot the man or woman of these studies, but what we choose to do with them. Ultimately, the ones echoes offer us a completely unique opportunity to explore the depths of our non-public soul and to higher apprehend who we're and the way our past reviews have lengthy-established our present lives.

For a few, the ones echo encounters may be a undertaking to their modern-day ideals and perceptions. For others, they'll be a affirmation of what they've got constantly identified in their coronary heart. Whatever your solution, I invite you to live open and curious. After all, the right charge of these memories lies now not in whether or no longer they may be virtually real or not, but within the this means that and records we can draw from them.

As the super novelist George Eliot advocated, "Our lives aren't most effective the existing, however additionally the beyond of which we are the product." Are you organized to discover your very personal recollections and the stories that have usual you?

As we are on this journey together, permit me provide you some examples of the way those encounters with beyond life echoes can take region in our each day lives. These are not really grandiose visions or profound goals, every so often the echoes can be diffused, almost imperceptible, and however on the same time as we stop to pay interest, they may screen profound truths about our souls.

Imagine, for example, on foot via a town you have got in no way visited earlier than, and however every street, every constructing, appears so unusually familiar. You may also even describe in element a monument or a landscape that you have not seen in your gift existence, however come what can also additionally bear in thoughts vividly. As we said earlier in Chapter 1, the ones are so-referred to as "cryptomnestic recollections," in which you undergo in thoughts data of a life you have not lived in this time and vicinity.

Or likely, you've got were given an unexplained worry of enclosed areas or heights, with out a disturbing experience in your modern-day-day existence that could provide an reason for this worry. As the famous psychiatrist Dr. Ian Stevenson recommended in "Twenty Suggestive Cases of Reincarnation" (1966), the ones unexplained fears may be echoes of disturbing opinions in a beyond lifestyles, a sort of emotional reminiscence that your soul has carried with you via time.

And what about those natural competencies that appear to come out of nowhere? Have you ever found your self drawing stunning sketches or gambling a musical tool simply, in spite of having no schooling within the ones areas? Perhaps, as Dr. Helen Wambach proposed in "Life Before Life" (1979), the ones talents are latent memories of skills and capabilities advanced in past lives.

These are only a few examples of approaches echoes from beyond lives can occur in our lives. And at the identical time as they may seem high-quality, they may be now not. Many people, in our quiet and introspective moments, have felt the caress of those forgotten recollections.

Now, highly-priced reader, you'll be asking yourself, "How do I recognize if those tales are absolutely echoes of beyond lives and not in truth my imagination prolonged lengthy past wild?" And it's far a valid query. Skepticism is healthy and a important part of our exploration. I inspire you to question, to look for evidence, to not receive smooth solutions.

But I may additionally say this: the price of those echoes lies now not so much of their foundation, but in what they'll be able to teach us about ourselves. These recollections, those flashes of over again, can be a powerful device for introspection and private boom. They can assist us understand our fears, our passions, our features.

So, are you organized to preserve this adventure, to delve deeper into the mystery and wonder of beyond lives? If so, be part of me on this adventure, due to the fact, ultimately, each step brings us toward the reality of who we genuinely are.

But, earlier than I move any similarly, permit me remind you all over again of a few thing.

Don't worry if the echoes are easy or far flung. Don't worry if the info are sharp or fuzzy. Clarity is not the purpose proper right here. Instead, allow's are searching out the reality of the revel in. As philosopher and poet Ralph Waldo Emerson wrote in "The Essay on Nature" (1836), "Truth is the assets of no man or woman, however it's miles the property of time." Perhaps, in our beyond lives, and in the course of this exploration, we can claim some of that belongings.

We have explored how visions and intuitions from our beyond lives can arise in our gift and the manner they may be a supply of introspection and personal increase. But what proof is there clearly for beyond life regression, and are there ancient and contemporary instances which could shed slight on this mysterious phenomenon?

My luxurious pal, I promise you that this adventure receives an increasing number of thrilling. In the following bankruptcy, we will study a number of the maximum fascinating and revealing instances of past-existence regression, each historical and cutting-edge-day. We will explore the recollections of people who, which include you and me, launched into this adventure thru the reflect of time, and positioned brilliant and transformative truths about their souls.

Are you intrigued thru the idea of analyzing greater approximately those testimonies and proof? Would you want to understand how those instances have recommended our expertise of beyond lives and their impact on our lives these days? If so, I invite you to join me on this journey of discovery. Together, we're able to remedy the mysteries of time and possibly, inside the approach, analyze a chunk extra about ourselves.

Are you ready to move on? Are you organized to keep to delve into this charming concern of past lives and all that it involves? Are you prepared to trade the way you view your existence, your soul, your purpose? If your answer is advantageous, then the following bankruptcy, "The Evidence for Regression: Historical and Contemporary Cases" is looking for you. There, we're able to delve into the substance of this thriller, into the coronary coronary heart of past lives. I am excited to maintain this journey with you. Are you equipped for the subsequent step?

Follow me, then, via the replicate of time, and permit us to discover together the secrets and strategies of the beyond, the echoes of the lives we've got got were given lived and the truths which can be although waiting to be located out. Remember, each step you are taking, each internet web page you turn, is one step toward understanding who you certainly are. Isn't that an adventure well worth taking? See you inside the next bankruptcy, my high-priced pal.

Chapter 15: The Evidence For Regression

There's nothing quite like the feeling of peering over the brink of the unknown, is there? That heady combination of interest, uncertainty and a chunk of pleasure that includes the promise of profound and probably transformative discovery. And proper here we're, you and I, repute on the edge of a modern precipice of understanding, equipped to plunge into the depths of past lifestyles regression.

But what if you had been to tell me that you want extra concrete proof? Evidence that transcends the location of hypothesis and summary questioning and lands firmly inside the realm of historic and contemporary testimony? Are you searching out that "Ariadne's thread" to help you navigate this labyrinth of facts?

You are inside the right vicinity, my friend. In this financial disaster, we're capable to speak about the evidence, the instances which have grew to come to be the concept of beyond lives from a metaphysical idea into a tangible, empirical reality. Both in records and in current-day times, there are memories of people who've skilled beyond existence regression in first-rate techniques and who have left verifiable proof in their reviews. From the bills of the historical Egyptians to the memories of our contemporaries, past life regression has been a constant state of affairs in human revel in.

As you technique this issue depend, you can discover your self questioning: How are we able to recognize if these memories are real? How are we able to distinguish reality from fable, reminiscence from creativeness? And, perhaps most significantly, what does all this propose for us as people on our personal adventure of self-discovery and non secular increase?

These are crucial questions, and to reply them, we need to dive deeper into the to be had evidence. So earlier than we circulate on, I need you to reflect on the subsequent: What are you seeking out in beyond life regression stories? Are you looking for evidence of the life of beyond lives, or are you seeking out a deeper understanding of your very own human revel in? Or, probable, are you seeking out each?

In this journey through time and space, I invite you to maintain an open mind. As Albert Einstein said in 1954 in his letter to Eric Gutkind, "The thoughts that is open to a cutting-edge idea will in no way cross again to its genuine duration." So, get prepared to increase your thoughts, my buddy, and permit me be your manual on this captivating journey through the facts and proof of past life regression. This adventure is as interesting as it's miles profound and I promise that, via the usage of the prevent, you could have won a cutting-edge diploma of understanding and appreciation of this superb detail of the human experience.

Are you equipped to dive into the captivating global of beyond life regression? Come, dive with me into this ocean of facts, and allow's swim collectively within the waters of historical evidence.

The phenomenon of past-existence regression, while it is able to look like a cutting-edge-day concept, has its roots firmly planted in antiquity. Historians have decided references to reincarnation and beyond lives in severa historic cultures, from the Celts to the Druids to the civilizations of India and China.

Take, for instance, the stories of historic Greece, wherein the philosopher and mathematician Pythagoras claimed to do not forget numerous of his beyond lives, alongside collectively with his life as a Trojan warrior in the mythical Trojan War. Pythagoras, first-rate stated for his mathematical theorem, turn out to be additionally a believer and practitioner of metempsychosis, an ancient Greek notion in reincarnation.

Now, I apprehend what you may be questioning, "That's captivating, however what approximately the extra present day proof? What about modern times of beyond-existence regression?" You are accurate, my pal. The modern-day evidence is truely essential to our statistics of this phenomenon.

This is wherein personalities which embody Dr. Brian Weiss, an eminent psychiatrist and author of "Many Lives, Many Masters" (1988), comes into the photo, recounting his enjoy with a affected person named Catherine, who under regressive hypnosis recalled more than one past lives that seemed to offer an purpose of plenty of her modern-day traumas and fears.

Another super example is that of Dr. Helen Wambach, a scientific psychologist from California who, within the Seventies, finished a sequence of experiments with regressive hypnosis. In her e-book Reliving Past Lives: The Evidence Under Hypnosis (1978), Wambach gives her findings, arguing that her subjects furnished accurate and verifiable info of earlier historic durations.

Cases of beyond-lifestyles regression also can seem wonderful, almost extraordinary at the start look. But if we permit ourselves to look beyond our regular belief, we can also additionally discover that those beyond-life debts are, in truth, evidence of a deeper and additional complicated fact than we typically expect. So I ask you: are you ready to project your assumptions and dive even deeper into the depths of the evidence for beyond lifestyles regression? If so, then permit us to pass forth, my brave fellow vacationer, into the exploration of the mysteries of time and the human thoughts.

The thriller and fascination surrounding past life regression isn't always restricted to anecdotal money owed and man or woman case studies. In truth, there have been a number of systematic research and research inside the place which have shed slight in this phenomenon from a broader attitude. Doesn't that sound exciting? Come on, dive with me into the wealthy tapestry of clinical proof and sudden discoveries that look in advance to you.

One such systematic have a look at emerge as accomplished with the aid of Dr. Ian Stevenson, a professor of psychiatry at the University of Virginia, who committed most of his profession to learning the past-life payments of youngsters. In his influential paintings "Twenty Suggestive Cases of Reincarnation" (1966), Stevenson documents a number of times of youngsters who regarded to don't forget data of beyond lives, data which have been later corroborated as correct.

Can you consider the surprise and amazement that the records told thru the ones children, which that they had no way of understanding, grew to grow to be out to be accurate? Doesn't that go away you in awe, complete of hobby and marvel at the large mystery of human existence?

One first rate case changed into that of a infant in Beirut, Lebanon, who remembered being a mechanic who died after being hit in the head with an axe. Stevenson modified into able to verify the information of the mechanic's existence and loss of existence that this toddler defined with first-rate accuracy.

Now, I understand this could be a chunk disconcerting, even unsettling. You also can discover resistance interior yourself to such debts, and that's ok. But I ask you to hold an open mind, to allow your self to explore those enigmas with out prejudice. Because, ultimately, we're in this adventure together, and an open mind is our best extraordinary buddy on this journey.

And speaking of adventures, what do you assert we delve even deeper into the captivating worldwide of scientific research on beyond lifestyles regression? Are you organized to head deeper, to preserve increasing the horizons of your information? If so, then permit's flow into on. I promise you which you are in for an interesting adventure.

After Stevenson, other researchers have found in his footsteps, searching out to delve deeper into this mystery. Dr. Brian Weiss, psychiatrist and author of "Many Lives, Many Masters" (1988), is taken into consideration one among them. Through his exercise, Weiss positioned that beyond-existence regression ought to have profound recuperation results, helping humans launch traumas and fears that seem to originate in beyond memories.

Although recognition of past life regression varies the diverse scientific and clinical community, it is clean that there's a growing body of evidence to indicate that there may be some element in these phenomena that deserves to be explored. Don't you find out it charming that, no matter all our differences, we're united by using manner of this consistent look for solutions, via this preference to understand what it means to be human?

We have journeyed together through this bankruptcy, exploring the evidence for regression: historical and present day times that have been examined, studied and documented. We have seen how beyond-lifestyles regression has been approached from particular views, and how compelling facts has been accumulated via numerous case research.

Together, we've got got opened our minds to new possibilities and stepped into the unknown, starting the door to new levels of know-how and reputation. Through this, my preference is that you have determined a extra statistics and deeper appreciation of the mysteries of human existence.

This, high priced pal, is best the start of our adventure. Soon we are capable of enter even more captivating territory. In the following economic disaster, we are capable of have a take a look at the enigmatic query of reincarnation, exploring historical philosophies and beliefs. We'll dive into the mysteries of time and life, and probably even ask some uncomfortable questions.

Are you ready to hold exploring the ones big mysteries with me, geared up to in addition open the door to expertise, to stand the unknown with braveness and curiosity? If so, then I invite you to preserve with me in this journey. I promise you it is going to be fascinating, tough and, drastically, deeply enriching.

Because, at the stop of the day, we aren't simplest right here to apprehend the mysteries of the universe, but also to recognize the mysteries of ourselves. And that, luxurious buddy, is the most captivating adventure of all. So, are you organized to hold? Come on, the journey awaits us!

Chapter 16: The Enigma Of Reincarnation

Have you ever puzzled why a few people and locations seem pretty familiar to you? Have you ever had the feeling that you have expert excessive quality situations in advance than? And I'm now not regarding that curious feeling of "déjà vu", but to some aspect deeper, extra rooted for your essence. In this monetary catastrophe, we're going to find out some thing that has captured the creativeness and curiosity of people given that ancient instances, some element that might offer solutions to these questions: the concept of reincarnation.

Reincarnation, as you apprehend, is the notion within the existence of successive lives, that the soul movements from one frame to each different in a cycle of start, loss of life and rebirth. But earlier than we dive into this first-rate ocean of records, I'd like to ask you a question: How do you notice lack of lifestyles: as an result in itself, a very final goodbye, or because the start of every extraordinary bankruptcy in the saga of your existence? As we find out together the historic philosophies and beliefs approximately reincarnation, I invite you to mirror on these questions.

Throughout the location, within the course of information, reincarnation has been a imperative concern of many philosophies and notion structures. From the historical cultures of Egypt and Greece to the religious traditions of India and Tibet, the idea that our souls live successive lives has been a mainstay.

In historic Egypt, as an instance, there has been a strong perception in the existence of an immortal soul. Funerary texts, together with the famous Book of the Dead, speak in element of the adventure of the soul after loss of existence and its eventual rebirth. Of path, as you could have observed on your journey via Chapter 2, those ideas are intertwined with the thoughts of karma and dharma, topics we are capable of address in later chapters.

And in historic Greece, the training of philosophers which consist of Pythagoras and Plato supplied reincarnation as a herbal machine of studying and evolution of the soul. Pythagoras, for example, remembered his past lives and saw reincarnation as an opportunity to purify the soul. Plato, alternatively, used reincarnation to give an purpose for the differences in abilities and potential between humans, suggesting that those variations had been the give up result of studies and know-how obtained in preceding lives.

But likely the most precise and complex reasons of reincarnation are determined in Eastern traditions, alongside facet Hinduism and Buddhism, wherein reincarnation and karma form the basis in their worldview. Have you ever wondered why Buddhists attempt so tough to acquire enlightenment? Or why Hindus speak about breaking free from the cycle of delivery and demise? In the subsequent a part of this financial disaster, we are capable of delve deeper into those traditions and find out how those ancient beliefs and philosophies can shed mild on our very personal beyond lifestyles research and recollections.

Let's communicate approximately Hinduism. In the Bhagavad Gita, one of the maximum sacred texts of Hinduism, the metaphor of converting garments is used to describe reincarnation: "Just as a person takes off his vintage garments and locations on a brand new one, so the soul takes to the air the antique body and puts on a present day one." (Bhagavad Gita, 2.22). Hinduism views life as an eternal cycle of starting, dying and rebirth, an without end turning wheel known as "samsara." Liberation from this cycle, or "moksha," is the last purpose of life.

Hindus furthermore agree with in the regulation of karma, a form of ethical law of purpose and impact, which determines an character's future in his or her next life. If you behave properly, do top deeds and fulfill your responsibilities, you're stated to accumulate notable karma, in case you want to purpose a extra favorable rebirth. On the alternative hand, awful deeds and terrible intentions gather awful karma, which could result in an poor rebirth.

Turning to Buddhism, we discover similar standards however with diffused versions. While Hinduism sees reincarnation as a transmigration of the soul, Buddhism speaks of "rebirth" in place of "reincarnation," and focuses greater at the continuity of interest than at the transmigration of an everlasting soul. According to Buddhist teachings, there can be no "self" or "soul" this is reborn, however rather a movement of hobby that continues, a succession of states of consciousness this is stimulated by way of karma.

The Buddha's teachings talk of liberation from this cycle of rebirth, known as "samsara," through the attainment of Nirvana. But Nirvana isn't always carried out absolutely by means of using collecting right karma, but rather via the whole eradication of preference, hatred and lack of know-how, the three "roots of evil" that, in step with the Buddha, bind us to the cycle of rebirth.

These historic philosophies and ideals provide us a wealthy tapestry of mind on reincarnation, however what do current-day philosophers and modern-day-day-day thinkers say? And how do the ones ideas resonate with our non-public past life critiques and reminiscences? Keep that hobby alive as we delve into the subsequent a part of our journey.

We will maintain our adventure via the meanderings of reincarnation ideals, however earlier than we drift on, I would really like you to take a second to mirror on what we have explored up to now. How do the ones thoughts resonate with you? Do you find out echoes of your non-public studies and recollections inside the ones historical philosophies? Remember, that is your journey, and those are the questions in an effort to deliver us closer to records the enigma of reincarnation.

Now, allow us to bear in thoughts the mind of a number of the current-day international's maximum influential thinkers on reincarnation. The British truth seeker and mathematician Bertrand Russell, as an instance, despite the truth that appeared for his skepticism, decided the concept of reincarnation quite possible. In his ebook "Mysticism and Logic" (1917), he cited that reincarnation, although it cannot be proved, can't be disproved each.

In addition, Carl Jung, a fantastic Swiss psychiatrist and psychoanalyst, famous for his principle of analytical psychology, become furthermore intrigued via the concept of beyond lives. Although Jung modified into now not overtly devoted to the concept of reincarnation, he explored the concept of the "collective unconscious," which suggests a shape of ancestral memory shared by using each person. Jung moreover recognized that goals and visions of past lives is probably an strive thru the unconscious to talk with reputation, a subject we are able to discover in addition in Chapter nine.

Another extraordinary instance is that of the American poet and fact seeker Ralph Waldo Emerson, who, in his essay "Compensation" (1841), counseled that if we remember lifestyles and dying as a chain of stages in a non-stop cycle, then "existence becomes a perpetual revelation of eternity...And reincarnation will become a opportunity."

These current-day thoughts approximately reincarnation regularly intersect with our very personal memories and intuitions of beyond lives. Consider, for example, the past lives you can have expert via goals, visions, or emotions of déjà vu. Could those be clues on your soul recalling research from preceding lives? After all, aren't anybody detectives of our very private souls, seeking out clues in our gift that would shed mild on our beyond?

As we replicate on the ones mind, allow me percent a touch anecdote. Once, in the route of a journey to the historical metropolis of Petra in Jordan, I became struck via the usage of an incredible experience of familiarity. Not most effective the points of interest, however the smells, the sounds, the whole lot appeared to job my memory of a few issue I had professional in advance than. Was it easy déjà vu, or became my soul recalling a past life in that ancient land? I do not know for sure, but what I do recognize is this journey made me mirror even more at the mysterious plot of reincarnation.

As we keep on our journey, bear in mind to preserve an open thoughts and a willing coronary coronary heart to find out the depths of your being. After all, because of the reality the Persian poet and mystic Rumi said, "We are not drops within the ocean, we're the ocean in a drop." In the remaining a part of this monetary damage, we are able to assessment the mind we've cited and set the diploma for the subsequent chapters.

And so, my pricey buddy, we've got navigated the waters of the enigma of reincarnation, exploring its philosophical and non secular depths, immersing ourselves in the thoughts of incredible thinkers and experiencing the possibility of remembering our personal beyond lives. It isn't an clean route, but like each extraordinary trips, it comes with its non-public rewards and discoveries.

Perhaps the quality discovery of all is that, in this sea of possibilities, we are all navigators, exploring the mysteries of the soul and reincarnation in our very private manner. Every memory, each instinct, every dream or imaginative and prescient of beyond lives we experience is a beacon, lights the manner to a deeper statistics of ourselves and our location within the cosmos.

As we navigate those waters, it's miles important to take into account that each oldsters has our own internal compass, and it's miles our right and duty to test that compass anyplace it leads us. As the philosopher Søren Kierkegaard stated, "Life can only be understood backward, however it want to be lived ahead." This quote encourages us to appearance to our past to understand our gift and, at the same time, maintain transferring toward our destiny.

Throughout this financial ruin, we've got got have been given positioned that reincarnation is an ancient however chronic idea that has worried and confused humanity for millennia. We have explored how unique cultures and religions during history have interpreted and carried out this idea, and the way current thinkers have pondered its viable veracity.

I thank you for joining me in this charming adventure via the enigma of reincarnation, and I hope you've got discovered some provocative thoughts and mind to help you replicate to your personal opinions and beliefs. But, hold in mind, that is handiest the start. There are however many mysteries to discover, many stories to inform, and lots of reminiscences to release.

In the following economic smash, "Scientific Revelations: Supporting the Past Lives Hypothesis," we're capable of develop our horizon and find out the diverse techniques in which modern-day-day-day technological know-how is contributing to our knowledge of the concept of past lives. From studies in fields as numerous as psychology, neuroscience and quantum physics, we're able to circulate beyond philosophy and theology to discover the empirical proof assisting the concept of reincarnation.

So, draw near your explorer's hat, prepare your open thoughts and consist of me on this journey via the replicate of time. I promise you it'll be a charming journey and you could test topics about your self and the universe which you have by no means taken into consideration earlier than. Are you organized? See you inside the next monetary catastrophe.

Chapter 17: Scientific Revelations

Welcome, my expensive reader, to each exceptional financial ruin in our immersive excursion through the twists and turns of the human mind and the mysteries of time. Have you ever had that eerie feeling that our our our our bodies and minds may additionally harbor reminiscences of lives we in no manner lived? Have you questioned if, at a few degree beyond recognition, our essence persists, collecting evaluations and facts in the route of multiple lifetimes? If so, then you definitely are within the proper region. In this financial disaster, we're capable of address a number of the medical breakthroughs that may shed mild on these vexing questions.

As we continue on our journey thru beyond existence regression, it is critical that we pause to keep in mind the era at the back of this phenomenon. In many approaches, technological understanding is the compass that enables us navigate this widespread ocean of enigmas and mysteries. And why, you may ask, is technology vital on this adventure? Isn't private revel in and individual beliefs sufficient?

Let me remind you, my buddy, that the motive of technological information isn't to confirm our beliefs, however to check them. Through rigorous assertion, experimentation and replication, generation lets in us to break up the wheat from the chaff, to determine amongst purpose truth and our subjective perceptions.

And it's miles proper here, at the edge of the unknown, wherein generation can be our first-rate first-class buddy. Scientific revelations provide us a unique attitude on reincarnation and past life regression. They allow us to test the claims, memories and proof from a rigorous and goal angle. They deliver us the opportunity to assignment our non-public ideals and prejudices, and ultimately assist us flow into one step toward the truth.

So what does generation say about the opportunity of beyond lives? Is there any goal evidence to useful resource the idea of reincarnation? Is there any medical studies on beyond lifestyles regression? What are the clinical motives for times of youngsters remembering beyond lives?

I invite you to find out these questions with me. Together, we're capable of take a journey thru some years of studies in fields as numerous as psychology, neuroscience, quantum physics and medication. At each prevent on our adventure, I will introduce you to studies and experiments that could shed mild at the thriller of reincarnation and past lives.

As we navigate the ones uncharted waters, I ask you to preserve an open thoughts, be willing to question your beliefs and be organized to face the wondrous complexity of the universe and the human mind.

So, organized for this fascinating adventure, my friend? Excellent. Get prepared to surf the waves of surprise, doubt, disbelief and, possibly, affirmation.

Because, in the long run, isn't always that what makes discovery so exciting? Our first port of call is a area you can now not expect to encounter on our voyage: quantum physics.

Quantum physics and reincarnation - what do they've in common? Well, likely more than you may think. Have you ever heard of quantum entanglement? It's a phenomenon that Albert Einstein as quick as defined as "spooky movement at a distance." You bear in thoughts Einstein, do not you? Author of the idea of relativity, one of the most tremendous minds of the 20th century, published in 1915.

In quantum entanglement, debris are related in the form of manner that the dominion of 1 right away impacts the country of the alternative, no matter the distance keeping apart them. Two debris may be mild years aside and although be "entangled". How does this relate to beyond lives?

Some have speculated that this phenomenon is probably the concept for the relationship amongst our past and gift lives. Perhaps our beyond life testimonies aren't "saved" in our thoughts or soul, however "intertwined" with them at the quantum diploma. Is this possible? Science has not however decided, but the mere concept of this possibility is already fascinating, do no longer you positioned?

Let us now flip to each other place that has furnished captivating evidence in useful resource of the past-existence hypothesis: highbrow research. One of the most genuine researchers in this vicinity is Dr. Ian Stevenson, who posted "Twenty Cases Suggestive of Reincarnation" in 1966.

For a long time, Dr. Stevenson and his colleagues on the University of Virginia have studied plenty of instances of kids who claim to do not forget past lives. Through meticulous detective artwork, they've sought to corroborate the claims of those youngsters, often locating specific records that appear to validate their recollections.

Of route, it's miles important to keep in mind that anecdotal proof, but compelling, does no longer constitute definitive evidence. But those studies actually upload an charming thread to the beyond-existence plot.

In addition, neuroscience has nowadays entered the conversation. With the development of mind imaging strategies, scientists can have a look at mind hobby in real time. This has made it possible to investigate whether or now not any extraordinary thoughts patterns exist within the path of past-existence regression periods. The consequences are provocative, to say the least.

I can see you're keen to study greater, and I don't need to disappoint you. So alter your compass, set your path for the horizon and get equipped for the subsequent leg of our journey. I'm superb what we can discover together can be captivating to mention the least.

Are you prepared to dive into the depths of the human mind? Here we bypass!

One of the maximum thrilling studies on this area grow to be done with the resource of way of Dr. Michael Newton, a hypnotherapeutic counselor and psychotherapist, whose ebook "Journey of Souls" (1994) has emerge as a landmark inside the literature of past lifestyles regression. Newton placed that in hypnotic regression instructions, a number of his patients commenced to undergo in thoughts reminiscences that seemed to go back from beyond lives.

Newton, at the start skeptical, have become intrigued via the ones steady testimonies and commenced out to investigate in addition. Through plenty of regression intervals, he amassed an extensive database of past-existence money owed and among-existence recollections which have interested readers round the sector.

Of path, it is critical to don't forget that, on the same time due to the fact the tales collected with the aid of Newton are interesting and frequently particular, they can not be considered "evidence" of the lifestyles of beyond lives inside the strict enjoy of the time period. They do, however, offer a body of proof that invitations further exploration and a wondering of our preconceived ideas approximately the character of interest and reality.

On some different the the front, Dr. Linda Backman, a psychologist and regression therapist, has studied the phenomenology of beyond-existence regressions for greater than a few years. In her ebook Souls on Earth (2018), Dr. Backman offers a fixed of nicely-documented instances that endorse the possibility of our souls residing more than one lives.

Meanwhile, neuroscience has supplied its non-public enigmatic findings. In a groundbreaking have a have a examine completed on the University of Virginia, researchers positioned that in regression instructions, wonderful areas of the thoughts, together with the hippocampus and amygdala, display a completely high stage of hobby. Is it possible that these thoughts areas are "gaining access to" past-life reminiscences?

In addition, a few neuroscientists have theorized that popularity can also additionally additionally exist independently of the mind and, therefore, need to preserve after bodily dying. This hypothesis, called "panpsychism," even though nevertheless debatable, indicates that popularity may be a crucial assets of the universe, like mass or electricity. If that were real, could not reputation then, in some shape, persist from one lifestyles to the subsequent?

As you may see, my friend, the waters of past lives are deep and complete of mystery. Although we are despite the fact that navigating the edges of the unknown, every discovery brings us one step toward know-how the last nature of our existence. Ready for the following leg of our journey? Good, because our subsequent holiday spot may be even extra charming.

Like intrepid navigators exploring the massive oceans of the unknown, you and I actually have traveled thru records, philosophy, and now, generation, looking for to get to the bottom of the mystery of past lives. We have considered the information gathered thru famend researchers along with Dr. Michael Newton and Dr. Linda Backman, and pondered the possible implications of the findings for the field of neuroscience. Every step of the way, we have stored an open mind, allowing the evidence to guide us, no matter wherein it may lead us.

It is time for us to take a short ruin in our journey to reflect on what we've got found up to now. We have located that the idea of past lives has been crucial to many philosophies and non secular traditions during facts. We have examined a number of the maximum captivating and properly-documented times of beyond-life recollections, and considered the possible implications of the medical proof supporting the reincarnation hypothesis.

Perhaps you find out yourself, like me, at the shore of this sea of know-how, with a enjoy of marvel and pleasure. Perhaps you furthermore mght discover yourself with a present day experience of opportunity, a spark of curiosity that drives you to discover beyond the regulations of our conventional understandings. And if it's miles the case, then I congratulate you, my buddy. For that is the sign of a true explorer's thoughts, the sign of a soul that refuses to sincerely take delivery of the unknown as not possible.

But, as you understand, our journey is a long way from over. We have explored the shallow waters of this giant ocean, but there are even more depths awaiting us. And in case you are recommended to transport on, I promise you that the treasures we are able to find out collectively may be more precious than all of the gold and jewels inside the worldwide.

What's in shop for us within the subsequent monetary disaster? Well, we're going to discover the intersection of psychology and regression, and be aware how the have a study of the unconscious can unlock the keys to our past lives. We're going to dive into the human mind, that excellent and mysterious inner universe, and who is aware of, probable we can find out a few secrets and techniques about ourselves along the manner.

So take a deep breath, my pal. And even as you are equipped, take the subsequent step in our adventure, into the unknown. I live up for seeing you within the next financial disaster.

Chapter 18: Psychology And Regression

Let me ask you a query, high priced reader: Have you ever confused how your mind works? No, I do now not mean the simple mind talents, however how your mind, emotions and goals are not unusual, how your feel of identity arises. Have you ever perception approximately that?

It is as though our mind have been a house with many rooms. Some are properly lit and resultseasily reachable; they will be in which we live most of the time. However, there are also those dark and forgotten rooms, full of recollections and feelings that we've pushed into darkness due to the truth they'll be too painful or disconcerting to confront inside the slight of ordinary cognizance. Those rooms represent what psychologists call the "subconscious."

Now, what if I advised you that the ones dark rooms to your mind may additionally encompass more than sincerely memories and feelings from this life? What if some of the ones closed doors bring about past lives, to tales and training your soul has accrued in its travels via time? Fascinating, isn't always it?

Well, that is precisely the idea we're able to find out in this bankruptcy: how psychology and regression can artwork together to explore the depths of our subconscious and release recollections of beyond lives.

Why is it important to find out the subconscious, you can ask. Well, first, it's miles critical to information ourselves. As the famous psychologist Carl Jung (1875-1961) as fast as said, "Until the subconscious becomes aware, it'll run your lifestyles and you'll call it destiny." In first rate phrases, to control our destiny, to live the lifestyles we desire, we should first realise and recognize the hidden forces that circulate us.

Second, by using the use of exploring our unconscious and the possible beyond lives stored in it, we are able to open a window into our soul, gaining a deeper revel in of who we're and why we are here. Psychology, in its quest to apprehend the human mind, and regression, in its try to hook up with our past lives, can be effective allies in this journey of self-discovery and personal increase.

And no longer pleasant that. As we're capable of show you on this bankruptcy, the combination of psychology and regression can provide a modern-day way to heal emotional wounds and treatment problems that have resisted one of a kind restoration techniques. In special phrases, this approach may be a powerful tool for non-public transformation.

So, are you geared up to find out the depths of your thoughts and loose up the doorways for your beyond lives? Are you organized to embark in this thrilling and transformative journey? Because, I promise you, this could be a journey like no specific.

Well, now that we understand what we're going to discover and why it is crucial, permit's begin to unpack the relationship among psychology and past lifestyles regression. To try this, we must begin from the start, from the element in which each disciplines meet: the subconscious.

The concept of the unconscious is taken into consideration one of psychology's most substantial contributions to human understanding. Carl Gustav Jung, a pioneer on this place, believed that the unconscious is a supply of facts and internal information. In his artwork, "Man and His Symbols" (1964), Jung emphasized the importance of desires, myths and archetypes in expertise the subconscious. For him, those symbolic photos have been a window to a deeper, ordinary truth, which transcends the character self.

If we bear in mind the possibility of past lives, those teachings of Jung tackle an entire new length. Rather than in fact symbolizing our personal dreams and fears, those pix of the subconscious can represent the opinions and classes of our souls in the end in their trips through time. In this manner, psychology will become a bridge that connects us with the statistics of our beyond lives and lets in us combine it into our present existence.

Now, how does beyond existence regression fit into all this? Well, regression is a way that allows access to unconscious reminiscences, which includes, constant with some practitioners, past life memories.

Brian Weiss, famous psychiatrist and creator of the notable-provider "Many Lives, Many Masters" (1988), is one of the maximum fervent proponents of this idea. In his ebook, Weiss recounts his revel in with a affected character, whom he named Catherine, who beneath hypnosis started out out to keep in thoughts episodes from what appeared to be beyond lives. According to Weiss, those memories allowed Catherine to loose herself from her fears and phobias, giving her a huge development in her present life.

If Weiss' revel in is any indication, past lifestyles regression can be a powerful tool for unlocking the recuperation potential of our subconscious. By permitting us to consider and analyze from our beyond lives, regression can help us heal emotional wounds, triumph over obstacles and better recognize who we are and what our purpose in lifestyles is.

I invite you to reflect on this. What studies, commands or revelations is probably equipped within the depths of your subconscious? What doors should you open in case you dared to discover your beyond lives? How can also your present existence alternate if you may do not forget and test out of your past reviews? Fascinating, isn't always it?

Now that we've got installed how psychology and past existence regression may be intertwined, it's time to move a step in addition and find out how this hyperlink is decided out in a practical setting. How does beyond existence regression genuinely have a have a look at in a recuperation putting and what advantages can it supply? To gather this, allow us to delve into the interesting case of an character, a middle-elderly guy we can name Robert.

Robert came to look a beyond-life regression therapist due to an excessive phobia of water that averted him from gambling water sports along together with his family and friends. Even a dip in a shallow pool changed into sufficient to purpose his panic. In his book "Regression Therapy: A Handbook for Professionals" (1990), writer Winafred Blake Lucas suggests that unexplained phobias can also have roots in disturbing beyond-lifestyles evaluations.

In remedy instructions, Robert emerge as subjected to a gentle hypnosis method geared towards assisting him lighten up and get admission to his subconscious. During the technique, colorful reminiscences emerged of a past existence in which he drowned in a shipwreck. Robert remembered despair, panic, bloodless water, massive waves and in the end darkness.

You can be asking yourself, and the way must I help Robert don't forget this sort of traumatic experience? Well, the mere act of remembering isn't the last aim. What without a doubt subjects is the way of integration and release that may be brought on by this memory.

Under the guidance of his therapist, Robert modified into able to face that ancient enjoy of drowning. By reliving his death in safe and controlled conditions, he modified into able to take away his fear, to allow it pass. Through this approach, Robert become able to understand that that life grow to be over, that he modified into secure now and that he did now not need to hold with him the concern of water from a past lifestyles. Over time and after severa periods, Robert have grow to be in a position to conquer his phobia. In the prevent, he even got here to enjoy water sports activities together along with his family and buddies.

Robert's case is surely one instance of techniques beyond life regression can be applied in a psychotherapeutic context to deal with problems that appear to have very little hyperlink to our contemporary lives. Now, I ask you, what do you believe you studied, isn't it fascinating to undergo in thoughts how exploring our beyond can free up our capacity within the gift?

Our adventure into the sector of psychology and beyond lifestyles regression is not yet over. There are extra wonders to discover, extra mysteries to treatment. So I invite you to hold going, to keep to delve deeper into this charming adventure. Because, in any case, we're exploring not best the beyond, however also our gift and, who's aware of, perhaps even our future.

So how does all of this suit into the huge picture? You have been quite affected person and receptive, and I'm certain you are obsessed with the opportunity of all that can be finished via psychology and past life regression. Robert's case is not any exception. In reality, there are various similar instances documented inside the scientific literature, suggesting that regression remedy can be a beneficial tool for addressing issues that can't be absolutely defined inside the framework of our contemporary existence.

In his ebook "Transformations in Consciousness: The Metaphysics and Epistemology" (1994), Ken Wilber, philosopher, psychologist and transpersonal theorist, explores how recollections of beyond lives can offer profound insights into ourselves and the research that shape us. We aren't sincerely discussing the possibility of preceding existences, however the large capability for non-public restoration and transformation that can get up from exploring those deeply rooted memories.

Now, I'm now not going to lie to you, the street may be hard. You can be confronted with memories and emotions that you had forgotten or might alternatively not don't forget. But do not worry, because of the truth you are not on my own in this adventure. Remember that there is normally a trusted therapist to manual you thru the ones recollections and help you discover this means that and peace in them.

Just because the waves preserve breaking at the shore, regardless of how first rate the limitations, we can also learn how to face and conquer our private fears and traumas, each from this lifestyles and previous ones. In doing so, we now not simplest discover recuperation and liberation, however we moreover come one step toward information the complex internet of reviews that make up our soul.

My friend, our adventure collectively on this bankruptcy is coming to an stop. We have explored the relationship amongst psychology and beyond lifestyles regression, and characteristic visible how this intersection may be a effective tool for restoration and self-discovery.

But don't worry, our adventure is a long way from over. In the following financial disaster, we are able to delve even deeper into regression therapy. We'll find out the way to take a guided journey into soul reminiscence, and possibly even get a glimpse into the wealthy and fascinating tapestry of our past lives.

So I invite you to maintain going, maintain exploring, preserve asking. After all, we are tourists in this massive universe of awareness, and every step we take brings us towards the truth. I sit up for seeing you inside the subsequent monetary catastrophe, with new adventures and discoveries. For every net web page we turn is a door that opens to a much wider universe of know-how.

Chapter 19: Regression Therapy

My buddy, in our previous encounters we have were given traveled collectively thru the labyrinth of lifestyles. We have explored thoughts, uncovered stories and dipped our ft inside the clean waters of records. Today, we preserve our adventure, venturing into terrain that guarantees surprises, discoveries and possibly even adjustments.

Are you organized to shed slight at the shadows of your reminiscence? If your answer is high quality, then you definitely definately are geared up to enter the area of regression remedy, that guided journey into the memory of the soul.

Regression remedy isn't always only a journey to past lives, it is a journey to the heart of your being, to that divine spark this is your soul. But why is that this adventure critical, why ought to we adopt it?

Imagine for a 2d which you are an archaeologist of the thoughts. Your vital device isn't a choose or a shovel, but your very own interest, your preference to realise, to recognize. You dig into your mind, looking for beyond recollections and research, humans who've left their mark on you, shaping your character, your behaviors and your ideals.

Now, keep in mind that you locate some factor to your highbrow excavation. It is not a physical item, however a reminiscence of a beyond life, a existence you lived a long time in the beyond, in a very unique region and at a awesome time. This reminiscence can be a key to expertise a number of the annoying conditions and issues you are going via to your modern-day life. Does this sound thrilling to you?

Let's circulate deeper: Why do you find out yourself interested in sure people and distanced from others? Why do a little situations seem familiar to you, regardless of the truth that you haven't skilled them in advance than in this lifestyles? Why do advantageous patterns repeat themselves again and again all over again to your lifestyles, no matter your remarkable efforts to alternate them?

The method to the ones questions can be hidden for your beyond lives. Regression remedy gives a completely unique opportunity to find out the ones recollections, to apprehend and in the long run heal the beyond life wounds that keep to influence your lifestyles in recent times.

Now, understanding all this, must you be interested in embarking in this adventure, delving into the depths of your soul and discovering the secrets and techniques and strategies and techniques that lie there? Remember, it is now not pretty lots curiosity or fascination with the beyond. It is set recuperation, growing, freeing yourself from antique chains and starting yourself to new possibilities.

Besides, you are not on my own on this adventure. Every step you take, every memory you discover, we will take collectively, constant inside the understanding that, regardless of what you come upon, I is probably here to accompany and manual you.

Think about it, expensive reader, what is going to you discover on this journey into the reminiscence of the soul? Are you organized to undertake it? If so, open your coronary heart to the opportunity of an exceptional adventure, full of surprises and wonders. Ready? Take a deep breath and dive into the exquisite worldwide of regression remedy.

Regression therapy is a subject full of opportunities, with a rich facts and a massive kind of strategies. However, simply as a painter wants to recognize the colors and palette earlier than portray his masterpiece, we need to recognize the fundamentals of this treatment to apprehend its healing capacity.

As the well-known psychologist Carl Jung should say, "He who appears outward, goals. He who seems inward, awakens" (Jung, 1943). (Jung, 1943) What is regression remedy if now not a manner to look inward, to rouse to a larger fact, to increase our focus beyond the bounds of the prevailing existence?

Regression treatment come to be pioneered inside the Fifties by means of manner of the usage of psychiatrist Morris Netherton. It is based totally on the concept that traumas and beyond lifestyles research can impact our current-day existence, affecting our emotions, conduct and physical fitness.

But how exactly does it art work? Think of your thoughts as a tremendous library. Every life you have lived is a book in that library. Through hypnosis and special techniques, a regression therapist will guide you to open the ones books and discover the recollections they incorporate.

Some of these recollections can be adorable and entire of pleasure. Others may be painful or tough to stand. But each one is a chunk of the puzzle of your soul, a key to understanding who you're and why you're right right here.

It have to be mentioned that no longer each person has the same opinion with the premises of regression therapy. Some critics argue that beyond-lifestyles recollections can be fantasies or delusions, the crafted from idea or the affected man or woman's imagination.

However, as Brian L. Weiss, author of "Many Lives, Many Masters" (Weiss, 1988) indicates, despite the reality that those reminiscences are figments of the creativeness, that doesn't decrease their recuperation price. If the ones "recollections" help us recognize and overcome our troubles, then why now not use them as a device for restoration and personal boom?

My pal, regression remedy is a fascinating adventure, but it isn't generally easy. It can take braveness to face the shadows of the beyond. But recall, every step you're taking on this journey is a step in the direction of a greater information of yourself and your soul's purpose. Are you ready to take the following step?

Now, allow's pass into a number of the better recognized regression treatment strategies and notice how those are implemented in workout.

Past Life Therapy (PLT), evolved via Dr. Roger Woolger in his e-book "Other Lives, Other Echoes" (Woolger, 1987), is one of the maximum considerably used strategies. PLT combines psychotherapy with regressive hypnosis and emotional release strategies to help clients explore and remedy difficult styles that seem to originate in past lives.

The crucial concept of PLT is that anybody carry with us the emotional and bodily wounds of our beyond lives, and that the ones wounds also can show up in our current lives as unexplained phobias, continual fitness troubles, or troubles in our relationships.

An example of the way this works in practice is probably the following: Imagine that you have an irrational worry of heights that has no explanation for your modern-day life reviews. Through regression therapy, you may discover a beyond life in which you suffered a disturbing dying through manner of falling from a exquisite peak. By coping with and liberating the trauma related to that enjoy, you could find out remedy out of your fear for your cutting-edge life.

Evolutionary Regression Therapy (ERT), developed through Dr. Michael Newton and defined in his ebook "Destiny of Souls" (Newton, 2000), is every distinctive important approach. Instead of focusing totally on past lives, ERT makes a speciality of what takes place among lives. In this "existence amongst lives," it is believed that our souls get higher, examine and plan for our subsequent incarnation.

ERT training are often prolonged, once in a while as an awful lot as 4 or 5 hours, and require a deep state of hypnosis. Clients who've expert ERT frequently describe it as a deeply religious approach that gives them a extra records of their existence cause and their location inside the cosmos.

Now, you might say, this all sounds amazing, but what evidence is there that the ones treatments paintings? Well, there are various testimonials from those who declare to have benefited from regression remedy. Some speak of bodily restoration, others of emotional launch, and others nonetheless of a profound feeling of peace and understanding. However, clinical proof is extra tough to acquire due to the subjective and intimate nature of those remedy plans.

Have you ever puzzled if regression remedy can be some detail for you? Could or not it's the crucial thing to unlocking the mysteries of your soul and starting off the door to a fuller, more enriching lifestyles?

Finally, within the spectrum of regression treatment, we find out Future Life Therapy (FLT), which, because the decision implies, specializes in future lives in place of beyond lives. Dr. Helen Wambach, a pioneer on this difficulty, completed a series of studies within the Eighties which have been later posted in her e-book "Future Lives: Advanced Projections" (Wambach, 1989). Through hypnosis, Wambach guided her topics to discover and describe their destiny lives, which, steady together along with her findings, have been remarkably regular in phrases of era, demographics, and cultural dispositions.

Of path, Future Life Therapy is not for every body. Like past lifestyles remedy, it can be unsettling and provoke existential doubts. But for individuals who are willing to discover the mysteries of their attention beyond the conventional barriers of time and area, it can provide precise and valuable insights.

In the journey of this bankruptcy, we've traveled from the acquainted terrain of our present existence to the unknown lands of our beyond and future lives. We have explored severa techniques and techniques, from Past Life Therapy (PLT) to Evolutionary Regression Therapy (ERT) and Future Life Therapy (FLT), every with its very own deserves and disturbing situations.

But like each journey, the most important detail is not the vacation spot, however what we studies along the manner. And this journey has clearly started. There is a whole lot greater to find out and discover within the captivating world of beyond life regression.

I'm high quality by way of the use of now, your interest has been piqued. Are you prepared to go beforehand and hold to get to the bottom of those mysteries? Ready to delve deeper into how goals can be a window into our beyond lives?

In the following chapter, we can discover the connection among desires and past lives. We will find out how our desires may be doors to past lives, and the manner we're able to learn how to interpret these wants to get to the bottom of their hidden messages. Isn't it interesting to think that each night time time, as we sleep, we may be touring to excellent instances and places, living one of a kind lives? I'll be seeking out you in the next bankruptcy to keep this interesting adventure. Until then, can also your dreams be candy and whole of mysteries to be unveiled.

Chapter 20: Emerging Memories

Imagine for a moment which you are repute on a beach. Your ft are buried inside the wet sand, and the sea wind is blowing gently in your face. The waves bypass step by step, every one leaving a white direction of foam in its wake. You watch within the distance due to the truth the solar, with its warm temperature orange glow, slowly dips under the horizon.

Now don't forget that each of those waves is a dream, and each dream is an echo of a past lifestyles. Isn't it charming how the sea of our thoughts can hold so many recollections and research that bypass past this existence?

Dreams are a general issue don't forget that has been with us while you consider that the start of time. In all cultures for the duration of information, goals had been seen as a mysterious territory that hyperlinks our normal worldwide with the unknown. From historic civilizations to fashionable neuroscience, desires have involved, involved and challenged mankind in its try to decipher their means that.

And on the identical time as dreams are frequently seen as mere constructs of our creativeness, it's miles exciting to ask: what if dreams are something extra than that? What if our desires are windows into our past lives?

It is at this captivating crossroads among desires and past lives that we find out ourselves in this financial ruin. If within the previous chapters we've examined the exciting idea of past lives, and explored how therapeutic regression can unencumber the ones hidden reminiscences in the soul's memory, we now embark on a dreamlike journey, in which we are capable of find out how dreams may be a manner to disencumber the secrets and techniques and techniques of our past lives.

Have you ever had a dream so vivid that it seemed like fact? Or a dream that left you with a sturdy revel in of déjà vu, as if you had been reliving a 2d out of your past, or even from a previous life? Those desires, my costly readers, can be more than just constructs of our imagination. They can be recollections developing from our beyond lives.

Exploring dreams as home windows into our past lives may also additionally appear like a modern day idea to many, however in truth, it has its roots in historical traditions and ideals. In ancient civilizations, which encompass the Egyptians and the Greeks, goals have been visible as divine messages, and had been perception to expose hidden truths approximately our beyond and destiny lives.

Are you equipped to embark on this journey thru desires and find out how they may be a window into your past lives? Are you organized to open yourself to the opportunity that the ones vibrant and mysterious goals you have got had can be extra than without a doubt fantasies of your slumbering mind?

Are you equipped to delve deeper into the area of your non-public dreams, into the confines of time and space, to find out who you had been to your past lives?

Let me quote the well-known Swiss psychologist and psychiatrist Carl Jung (1875-1961), author of numerous influential works together with "Dreams, Memories, Reflections" (1962). Jung believed that dreams are a form of verbal exchange with our subconscious. But even more fascinating, he claimed that there are positive desires, which he known as "archetypal desires," that skip beyond our non-public experience and may have their foundation in past lives. According to Jung, the ones archetypal desires may additionally additionally consist of symbolic elements that recur inside the path of awesome cultures and eras, suggesting a commonplace connection to all humanity, a collective memory, which he known as the "collective unconscious".

Let's keep in mind an example. Imagine you dream you are in an historic Roman market, searching for olives and spices. You can scent the smells, pay attention the bustle of humans, and sense the warmth of the solar on your pores and pores and pores and skin. Although you've got in no manner been to Rome on this lifestyles, now not to say historic Rome, to your dream you experience at home. This dream might be a acquire of your creativeness, inspired thru a movie you observed or a e-book you have a take a look at. But it could additionally be an rising memory from a beyond lifestyles.

This concept is supported thru present day research in the place of transpersonal psychology, which indicates that a few dreams can be beyond-lifestyles reviews. Psychiatrist Brian Weiss, writer of the bestseller "Many Lives, Many Masters" (1988), is one of the maximum incredible proponents of this idea. Weiss has documented severa times of patients who, through regression treatment, have recalled beyond lives in their dreams.

Now, you'll be questioning, how can we distinguish among an normal dream and a dream that is a reminiscence of a past life? There isn't any definitive option to this query, however there are superb trends that might advise that a dream can be a past life revel in. These dreams are usually extraordinarily extremely good and precise, and are frequently found with the aid of the usage of sturdy feelings. In addition, they may consist of accurate ancient elements of which the dreamer had no previous data.

Let me ask you one extra query: Have you ever had a dream so real, so unique, that you wakened with a experience of surprise and awe? A dream wherein you could scent, touch and sense as if you have been truely there? If so, likely you were glimpsing a reminiscence of a beyond lifestyles.

However, this concept is not with out controversy. Some scientists argue that dreams aren't anything greater than the end result of mind interest sooner or later of sleep, and not the use of a connection to beyond lives. However, we can not deny the numerous recollections of people round the region who speak of goals that seem to include echoes of beyond lives.

Let me percent with you one such tale, one that I truely have commonly placed in particular thrilling. This story is of a person named James, who, from a more youthful age, started having habitual goals approximately the life of a fighter pilot throughout World War II. In his dreams, James can also need to look extensively specific records, from the types of plane getting used to the names of the guys he became flying with. When James determined to research the ones dreams, he emerge as surprised to find out that the whole lot he had seen in his desires matched historic reality. Coincidence? Or an emerging memory from a beyond existence?

Or recollect the case of Jenny Cockell, author of Across Time and Death: A Mother's Search for Her Past Life Children (1993). From youth, Jenny had remarkable, normal dreams approximately the life of an Irish lady named Mary who died leaving in the back of numerous more youthful kids. Driven through a need to locate the ones kids, Jenny set out on a quest that finally led her to reunite with Mary's now-aged kids in real existence.

These memories mission us to rethink what we realise approximately desires and beyond lives. They invite us to open our minds to the opportunity that our desires can be greater than simply constructs of our imagination.

I ought to tell you, my reader friend, that studies on goals and past lives stays in its infancy. We do now not have all of the solutions, however each day we're learning greater about this captivating phenomenon. What approximately you, are you inclined to explore your dreams with an open mind, to don't forget the opportunity that they will be home home windows into your past lives?

Before transferring on, I may want to no longer want to overlook the detractors of this idea. Among them is psychologist and cognitive scientist Steven Pinker, author of "How the Mind Works" (1997), who argues that goals are certainly the crafted from a "mind in a country of rest." According to Pinker, desires are mere byproducts of brain interest for the duration of sleep, without a connection to beyond lives or reincarnations. Yet even Pinker admits that we do now not honestly recognize the thriller of desires.

Therefore, despite the reality that theories about the connection among desires and beyond lives are debatable, we cannot disregard them. Dreams are a ordinary revel in, shared by using every body in some unspecified time in the future of records. Could or now not it's far that this wellknown revel in additionally connects us to our past lives?

In the stop, expensive reader, the selection is in your hands. You have the choice to dismiss those standards as mere fantasies, or you can pick out to discover them with an open mind. As constantly, I invite you to do your private studies, have a look at your instincts and find out your personal solutions. No recall in which your path takes you, I am right here to accompany you each step of the manner, sharing with you the wonders and mysteries of past lives.

www.ingramcontent.com/pod-product-compliance
Lightning Source LLC
Chambersburg PA
CBHW071445080526
44587CB00014B/2000